CW01551293

FORESTS OF DEATH

Legion of the Damned Book Two

Jeff Jones

SAPERE
BOOKS

FORESTS OF DEATH

Published by Sapere Books.

24 Trafalgar Road, Ilkley, LS29 8HH

saperebooks.com

Copyright © Jeff Jones, 2025

Jeff Jones has asserted his right to be identified as the author
of this work.
All rights reserved.

No part of this publication may be reproduced, stored in any
retrieval system, or transmitted, in any form, or by any means,
electronic, mechanical, photocopying, recording, or otherwise,
without the prior written permission of the publishers.
This book is a work of fiction. Names, characters, businesses,
organisations, places and events, other than those clearly in the
public domain, are either the product of the author's
imagination, or are used fictitiously.
Any resemblances to actual persons, living or dead, events or
locales are purely coincidental.

ISBN: 978-0-85495-746-0

For Gavin and Becky

ACKNOWLEDGEMENTS

It has long been a dream of mine to see Centurion Corvo and his comrades march out of my already over-populated head and onto the page, and I would like to place on record my sincere thanks to Natalie Linh Bolderston whose editing skills have helped to transform my scribblings into another book I can be proud of. My thanks also to Caoimhe O'Brien and everybody else behind the scenes at Sapere Books whose tireless work has made this dream a reality.

My gratitude also to everybody who has supported me over the years and provided invaluable feedback and encouragement, including my family and all the short story writers and editors I have had the pleasure of interacting with.

Most of all though, my undying thanks to you the reader without whom the Legion of the Damned could not enjoy the adventures they have already and the ones to come.

CHAPTER 1

Germania, winter AD 59

They were going to be slaughtered.

Centurion Vitus Jovian looked around at his remaining men. A small detachment of heavy infantry from the Twenty-Second Legion based in Fort Duma, one of three wooden forts on the northern side of the Rhenus, the men had put up a ferocious defence. The number of dead and wounded enemy warriors who lay on the ground was testament to that. There would be many funeral pyres in their village tonight. Jovian would do his best to see their numbers swell yet further before he drew his last breath.

He tried to turn, but his right foot wouldn't move. He looked down in disgust at the mud that clung to him. With great effort he finally managed to tug his foot free, and he took a few steps to his left, where he hoped the ground was a little firmer. It had rained continually for days, turning much of the forest into a mud bath. The clearing in which Jovian and his men now stood didn't have the benefit of tree cover and consequently the ground was saturated, treacherously so, and he was sick of it. In fact, he was sick of the whole damned place with its seemingly endless forests, damp climate and hostile barbarians. It was a mystery to him why so many emperors had sought to add this cesspit of a land to the Empire.

Shaking his head, Jovian looked at the bodies in front of him. Most of them were tribesmen, but many were his men. Too many. Yes, they had put up a brave fight and he was proud of them — not that he'd ever tell them to their faces — but the final outcome was inevitable. In the end, the weight of numbers would prevail. In his considerable experience, it usually did.

He faced his men, noting their anxious expressions. Now in his late forties and considerably stockier than when he had first enlisted, Jovian recognised himself in some of the scared faces before him. He removed his helmet and fiddled with the red crest that signified his rank of centurion. Then, after wiping the rain from his forehead and eyes with the back of his wrist, he placed his helmet back on his head and tightened the strap.

"Well fought, men. We gave these bastards a hard battle, but there's just too many of them. One last effort, though, eh? Form square!" The last two words were spoken with more force.

It was a manoeuvre they had practised countless times on parade grounds across the Empire. Even under the stress of battle, they quickly and effortlessly assumed the new formation. After casting an appraising eye over his men and ordering a couple of them to tighten the shield wall, Jovian took up a position at the centre of the square, from where he could see everything and everyone.

He turned his gaze to the edge of the small clearing, where the tribal warriors were busy summoning the courage for another assault. Many of their fathers, brothers and sons lay dead or dying in front of the hated Romans and many more would die in the next attack, but today their victory was close. They knew it and Jovian knew it. All they had to do was bravely throw themselves at the beleaguered Romans one last time and they would prevail.

A veteran of many battles and campaigns, Jovian was nearing the end of his time serving the Eagles. On completion of his service, like all veterans, he had expected to be granted a parcel of land somewhere in one of the conquered provinces. In quieter moments back in the fort, he had imagined himself taking a plump wife from the local population wherever he ended up. She would have wide hips and would bear him many children. He would run a smallholding with some animals and crops. He would be content, perhaps even happy. When his children grew up and provided him with grandchildren, he would sit by the hearth and tell them stories from his days in the legions. Some of them might even be true.

Now, as he stood proudly at the heart of what remained of his men and stared out over the wall of shields at the snarling warriors just a short distance away, he knew that dream would never be realised. Instead of seeing out his days in the warm sunshine of some far-off province, his body would be left to rot in this wet and miserable barbarian forest, food for carrion, his name and deeds lost to the mists of time. He'd be just another son of Rome sacrificed needlessly for the vanity of an emperor he had never seen. This is where his story ended.

The jeers and roars from the enemy had reached fever pitch, and Jovian sensed that they had finally worked up enough courage to launch a fresh attack. It would soon be over.

He transferred his gladius from his right hand to his left and surreptitiously wiped his sweating palm on his cloak before returning his gladius to his favoured hand. He needlessly straightened his helmet, a ritual he had started just before some long forgotten battle, and nodded in resignation. He would not die cheaply, and he would not allow himself to be taken prisoner. Everyone knew how the traitor Arminius and his Germani tribesmen had tortured any Roman officers and centurions they had captured after the Battle of Teutoburg Forest exactly fifty years earlier. He did not intend to suffer the same fate. Realising the battle was lost, rather than be captured, General Varus and his senior officers had taken their own lives, leaving their men to fight on alone with nobody but junior officers to lead them. It had been a slaughter and cost Rome three of her best legions. Varus' name, along with that of Arminius, was still cursed to this day.

If it came to it, Jovian would also take his own life, but not while his men lived and fought. He would not abandon them in such a cowardly way.

A final roar from the tribesmen sent the crows into a panicked flight from the tall trees surrounding the clearing, and then they charged.

"Steady now, men. Hold your formation," urged Jovian in a voice he hoped didn't betray his fear. Despite the cold of the Germanic winter, the hand holding his gladius once again felt sweaty. To his dismay, a never-ending stream of tribesmen was rushing out of the treeline towards them. It didn't matter how many of them they killed, there always seemed to be more. "Brace!" he roared when they were no more than twenty strides from his men.

It was then that something completely unexpected happened. Peering above the iron rims of their shields, his men watched as a score of the tribesmen who had been racing towards them were suddenly knocked off their feet by what looked like a volley of Roman javelins. The tribesmen's advance continued, albeit at a slower pace, but when a second volley slammed into their ranks a few heartbeats later, their attack ground to a confused halt.

Jovian turned to look behind him and was surprised to see between forty and fifty men standing in the treeline. Most wore Roman uniforms, but others were dressed more like the locals, and he assumed they were auxiliaries. Whoever they were, they were a gift from Mithras and most welcome.

A young centurion with an older-looking man of indeterminable rank standing next to him, shouted for his men to charge. Still standing at the centre of the square, Jovian watched as the new arrivals rushed past his men and started to attack the bewildered tribesmen. Those not dressed as Roman legionaries fought without discipline and with a savagery that shocked Jovian, though he could not deny its effectiveness. These men had clearly never served in the legions and were probably auxiliaries drawn from the farthest reaches of the Empire.

"Well, what are you waiting for, men? Attack them!" ordered Jovian, and without a moment's hesitation, his men broke the square and raced to join the battle.

Shocked by the sudden appearance of these new Romans and unsure of how many more were hiding, many of the tribesmen were already looking to disengage and flee to the safety of the trees. Some of their braver comrades turned to face this new threat. Victory had been within their grasp, and now they were on the verge of defeat.

Jovian was about to join the fray when the sound of footsteps drew his attention. He turned to find the young centurion and the older man standing just behind him.

"I don't know who you are or where in Hades you just came from, brothers, but I'm very happy to see you," Jovian greeted.

"I am Centurion Marcus Ovidius Corvo, and this is Cornelius Arus from Legate Crispus' staff," said the young centurion as he nodded towards his older companion and offered his hand to Jovian. They clasped arms and smiled at one another.

"Centurion Vitus Jovian, eighth cohort of the Twenty-Second Legion." Jovian released Corvo's arm and clasped Arus' in the same fashion as he studied the older man's face. "I've heard of you. The legate has mentioned you often."

"It's good to know that he still remembers me."

"I'm sure seeing you again will raise his morale, for there has been little cheer about these parts for some time," said Jovian mysteriously before turning his gaze back to the battle taking place in front of them.

The fighting was largely over, most of the tribesmen having melted back into the dark forest they called home, but here and there isolated warriors fought bravely on. The three men watched as a burly tribesman with a huge axe swung his weapon in a powerful arc at the man in front of him. His opponent nimbly ducked under it before slashing the axe-wielder across the back of his thigh with his gladius. The tribesman howled with pain before turning astonishingly quickly for such a big man and swinging his axe at neck height. Again the other man avoided the arc of the axe, this time by arching his back. The weapon sliced through the air, no more than a hand's breadth away from decapitating him. Quick as a flash, the man straightened and thrust forward with his gladius. The tribesman had somehow anticipated the move and managed to twist evasively, but the gladius blade still pierced his side, the thick bearskin he was wearing preventing the blade from penetrating too deeply. The tribesman placed a hand over the wound and then studied the bright red blood on his palm. He grunted, wiped his hand on his bearskin and then grasped his axe, the wound seemingly no more than a minor irritation to him.

The two men circled one another for a few moments, watching for weaknesses and vulnerabilities. Eventually the tribesman's patience expired and roaring a battle cry, he launched himself at the Roman, swinging his axe with frightening speed. A huge downward chop designed to split the Roman in two was only just avoided after he slipped on some mud slick with blood and landed heavily on his back. Rolling quickly onto his side, the Roman stared wide-eyed as the axe head slammed into the space where just moments before his head had rested.

The thick mud clung to the axe head, sucking the blade deep into the ground. As the tribesman struggled to tug his weapon free, the Roman rolled behind him and sliced the back of his ankles. The big warrior cried out in pain and collapsed to his knees, his weapon finally free of the mud. Unable to see the Roman behind him, he swung his axe wildly back and forth until a powerful kick sent him sprawling into the mud face-first. The Roman was on him in an instant, pinning the man to the ground with a foot between his shoulder blades. Then, with all the strength he could muster, the Roman plunged his gladius down into the base of the man's neck. The tribesman's body twitched a couple of times and then went still.

As Jovian and the others watched, the Roman pushed his gladius back and forth as if trying to free his blade from deep inside the tribesman's neck, but it was only when he stood and roared, holding the fallen man's bloody head aloft, that his true intention was revealed.

It had the desired effect. Those tribesmen that had not yet fled and were able to do so looked at the head of their comrade and then turned and ran for the trees. Those still fighting either tried to quickly end their duel or simply turned to run and in doing so, exposed their backs. All were cut down and none were permitted to escape. Neither were the wounded; they were all put to the sword, neither Corvo's nor Jovian's men inclined to show mercy.

"Are all the men under your command that good at fighting?" asked Jovian, shaking his head in admiration of what he had just witnessed. "I wouldn't have wanted to tackle the big man with the axe."

"The man who killed him is one of the best, if not the best of my men," said Corvo proudly.

"Your men? I thought…" Jovian didn't finish his sentence as he turned to face Arus.

"Centurion Corvo commands here, Centurion Jovian. I am merely along as a facilitator," replied Arus.

Jovian had questions but decided that it was neither the time nor the place to voice them. Instead he said, "Your men are…"

"Undisciplined? Wild?" asked Corvo.

"I was going to say 'unique', but yes, that would also perhaps describe them. I've never seen a legionary fight like that before."

"That's because that man is Atilus, and he is no legionary."

"Atilus? The gladiator who won his freedom?" Jovian asked, and Corvo nodded. "That would explain it, then. And the rest of your men, are they also gladiators?"

"Some. Others are legionaries, and some are prisoners we've borrowed from prisons and quarries."

Jovian's eyebrows climbed so high that they briefly disappeared beneath his helmet. "It sounds like you have an interesting story to tell, and I'd be glad to hear it if you're so minded?"

"I don't see the harm in that, but not now, not here. Now, I think it best if we try and put some distance between ourselves and this place in case your friends come back," said Corvo.

"I don't think there's much likelihood of that, certainly not today, not after what your men have just done. They'll run off home back to their camp, tell everyone what happened here and drink themselves into a stupor as they try to restore their courage. Then they'll come looking for us, but by then we'll be safely behind the fort's walls."

"How far to where the legate is based?" asked Arus.

"We're spread across three forts. The nearest one is Fort Duma, where me and the men are stationed, then the legate is based at Fort Felix a half day's march to the west. The same distance to the west of Felix stands Fort Otto. We'll make it back to Duma before it gets dark, but you'll have to stay there overnight. It's not a senator's villa, you understand, but better than what you've been used to of late, I'm sure. Then I'll get someone to take you to Fort Felix in the morning. Does that sound all right?"

"A fire, a bunk, hot food and a roof over our heads? You have no idea how welcome that sounds right now, Centurion," said Arus. "The damp of this wretched place has already got deep into my bones."

"Better get used to it, sir, if you plan on staying here for very long. When winter comes and the snow starts to fall, you'll find yourself wishing for balmy days like this."

The look of horror that spread across Arus' face made both centurions grin.

A Roman soldier came striding over to where the three men were standing and snapped smartly to attention before saluting.

"Beg to report, Centurion, all enemy have retreated, and any wounded have been despatched with Rome's compliments," he said, addressing Corvo directly.

"Thank you, Optio. Have the men form up, please. We will march behind Centurion Jovian's men, who will be leading us to a nearby fort where I am assured there will be bunks and hot food for everyone. You may tell the men that."

"Thank you, sir. The men will be pleased to hear that, I'm sure." The optio saluted again, nodded at Arus and Jovian and then strode away, barking orders for the men to form up. He sweetened the command with promises of food and bunks; it had the desired effect, and the men were soon lined up accordingly.

"Was that…?" began Jovian.

"Optio Sextus Nerva from the training grounds outside Rome? Yes," answered Corvo.

"Gladiators, prisoners, drill masters — your tale grows more intriguing by the moment. Optio Valus!"

"Sir?" said one of Jovian's men, who came striding over when he heard his name. He snapped to attention and saluted every bit as smartly as had Nerva.

"Have the men fall in, Optio. We'll be escorting these men to Duma, and I want to make best time, but make sure the men remain vigilant. Those hairy-backed barbarians are unlikely to show their faces again today, but we'll take nothing for granted."

"Yes, sir." The optio saluted and then hurried away to carry out his orders.

CHAPTER 2

The journey to Fort Duma took the rest of the afternoon. The men marched through its wooden gates under the watchful gaze of its garrison just as dusk arrived, bringing with it a depressingly early darkness. As soon as the last man was through, four legionaries lifted the heavy oak beam back into place, sealing the gates to the outside world, or so they hoped.

Fort Duma was a small fort with wooden palisades and steps which led down to the main square. Several simple wooden buildings with turf roofs served as the barracks, officers' quarters and mess room, with other smaller buildings designated as a medical bay, a storeroom and briefing room. To help new men settle into their postings, all forts and camps across the Empire were laid out in exactly the same fashion regardless of their size, and this one was no exception.

When everyone had reached the centre of the square, Jovian called the column to a halt. Most of the fort's garrison had gathered to watch. Jovian knew they would be speculating as to the identity of the new arrivals, or seeking out friends and finding some missing. A murmur of discontent spread through the gathered men, but Jovian chose to ignore it. Glancing round, his gaze settled on two young legionaries and before they could make themselves scarce, he summoned them to him.

"As you two seem to have nothing better to do than stand there staring, you can show these men where they can bunk down." He waved in the general direction of Corvo's men. The two legionaries looked at them open-mouthed, obviously trying to work out where they were going to manage to find billets for so many men. Jovian rolled his eyes. "There are bunks free from the men transferred to Fort Otto, and I'm sure it hasn't escaped your notice that not all of the men came back from our patrol, so they won't be wanting their bunks anymore either. Put all our men in one block and these new men in another. Some of ours will moan, no doubt, so if there are any problems, find Optio Valus and get him to intervene. Got it?" The two young legionaries nodded, but Jovian wasn't convinced. Optio Valus was probably in for a difficult evening and would soon be cursing his name. "Well, you have your orders." The two legionaries jumped to attention, saluted and nervously made their way to the group of tough-looking men who had accompanied the centurion through the gates.

Some of the garrison were watching the newcomers with interest, others with borderline hostility. Some were discreetly pointing and whispering to their comrades.

Jovian turned to the men who had returned from patrol with him. "Well done today, men. It was tough out there. Go and get yourselves something to eat and drink and toast our fallen brothers. Dismissed." The men all came smartly to attention and then broke up into small, weary groups, heading for the barracks and mess room. Jovian turned to Corvo. "Right, I have room in the officers' barracks for three only, I'm afraid."

"That will be Cornelius Arus, Tribune Gaius Crispus and myself," said Corvo.

"Tribune Crispus?" asked Jovian, his eyebrows disappearing into his helmet once again.

"Yes, we have the legate's son with us."

"But he's not in command either?"

"No."

"I've obviously been in this backwater too long. The legions clearly aren't what they used to be, what with gladiators and freed prisoners among their ranks, and tribunes subordinate to centurions. No offence."

"None taken," said Corvo with a smile. "And I can assure you that our circumstances are … unique."

"So it would seem. Well, who am I to question the wisdom of my betters? Now, if you care to follow me, I'll show you to the best accommodation this side of the Rhenus," said Jovian, laughing at his own joke.

Two hours later, Corvo, Arus, Crispus and Jovian sat around a brazier drinking wine as the wind outside howled and rattled anything not properly nailed down. Arus drew his cloak around his shoulders and shuffled nearer to the brazier. They had all enjoyed a hot stew consisting of an indeterminable meat, some bread, and a slice of cheese, and the stresses of the day were seeping away. As Jovian had feared, not all of his men had taken kindly to being ordered to move to another barrack block and he had eventually been summoned by a runner sent by Optio Valus. An argument had broken out and was on the verge of escalating. Although he had stormed over brandishing his vine cane, a centurion's mark of rank, in the end he had been able to resolve the issue peacefully. The man causing the majority of the trouble was in fact upset and angry at the loss of his best friend earlier that day on Jovian's patrol. His forced relocation to another barracks had just given him an excuse to vent his anger. Jovian had been lenient with the man.

"All sorted over in the barracks, then?" asked Corvo when Jovian had returned and set about pouring more wine into everyone's cups.

"Yes, nothing more to worry about."

"I appreciate you and your men being so accommodating."

"Don't mention it."

"Centurion Galba and Optios Flavius and Nerva are bunking with my men, so they won't cause any problems, I can assure you — not unless they want to get on the wrong side of that trio."

"No, Centurion Galba is a big man, but then most of your men look as if they can handle themselves."

"Believe me when I say they can."

"Which leads us nicely to your tale. My watches are posted and I'm not due to do my rounds for some time yet, so why don't you tell me how it is you come to be here?" suggested Jovian.

And so they did. Corvo told most of the story, with Arus interjecting every now and again and Gaius adding his perspective from when he entered the timeline. When he had finished telling the story, ending with them stumbling across Jovian and his men being attacked by the Germani tribesmen, Jovian was staring back at him in astonishment.

Corvo laughed. "Your surprise makes me wonder if I have embellished the story, but actually I have probably played it down. Our true storyteller is my optio and good friend, Lucius Flavius."

Jovian nodded, remembering the man he had seen enforcing Corvo's orders. "Well, I've served the Eagles for just over twenty-three years, and I've seen and taken part in a lot in that time, some of which I'm not proud of, but your tale surpasses it all. So let me get this right: the legate, your father —" he looked at Crispus, who nodded in response before Jovian turned to Arus — "ordered you, Arus, to pick a man to lead a rescue mission deep into Armenia, where Tribune Crispus was being held captive, along with several other men?" Arus nodded. "And you, Marcus —" he looked at Corvo — "were selected to lead this suicide mission because you were expendable?"

"I think it's safe to say that I was in the wrong place at the wrong time," Corvo replied with a sigh. "My foolish actions rendered me vulnerable."

"And this is because while serving under the legate on the Dacian border with the Eleventh Legion, you broke ranks and attacked the enemy, leading to a counter-attack by our men, which eventually turned the battle? But instead of being punished, you were ordered to lead this rescue mission?"

"That's right," Corvo confirmed.

"But they wouldn't give you a legion or anything? Instead you had to recruit your own men and save for a handful of willing or perhaps deranged legionaries, you had to recruit from the gladiator schools, prisons, mines and quarries?" continued Jovian.

"Yes," replied Corvo.

"Then you marched and sailed halfway across the known world, went deep into enemy territory where, dressed as natives, you were just as vulnerable to attack from your own side as you were the enemy. There you rescued the tribune and a handful of others, even finding the time to help in the defence of a frontier fort on the way home just for good measure. Then you find the legate has been redeployed to the Rhenus area, and have traipsed all the way here to find him. Does that cover everything?"

Corvo and Arus looked at one another, grinned and then nodded.

"There were other obstacles thrown in our path along the way, but yes, that just about sums it up. Strictly speaking we cannot tell anybody about it, present company excepted. Oh, and other than my men being granted pardons and their freedom, we will never receive any recognition for what we did, although the legate has promised to pay them handsomely in silver."

Jovian shook his head. "A feat like that should be worthy of a triumph like they used to do in the days of Caesar and Pompey."

"The centurion knew the conditions when he accepted the mission," said Arus, downing the last of his wine.

"You make it sound as if he had a choice in the matter," said Jovian.

"Oh, he did. Accept it willingly or accept it reluctantly."

"Well, I for one will be forever grateful to Marcus and his Damned," said Crispus, raising his cup in salute. "I don't know how much longer I could have survived there."

"The Damned?" asked Jovian.

"It is the name the men have chosen for themselves — the Legion of The Damned," replied Corvo.

"Given that your force consists of gladiators, slaves and prisoners, I would say that seems a fitting name, if not a little dramatic. So what is next for you?"

"Tomorrow, we will finally reunite Gaius with his father, collect the pardons for my men and then they will be disbanded. The regular men among us will no doubt either return to their units or be redeployed by the legate."

"And yourself?"

Corvo frowned. "I do not know."

"Well, I must warn you, and I beg your pardon for my bluntness, Tribune, the legate is not the man he once was, certainly not the man I knew when I served under him a few years ago. You already know that he was apparently sent here as the emperor had become jealous of his successes and wanted him far enough away from Rome that he could not cause the emperor any problems?" The others all nodded. "Well, things have not gone well for him here either. It was a fairly peaceful sector around here until the legate arrived and started sending patrols out. Before, the tribesmen left us alone and we largely left them alone. The patrols changed things, though, and provoked the tribesmen. They started attacking our patrols, nothing too serious, just reasserting their ownership of the forest, but of course we'd then have to go out and seek revenge. Things just spiralled from there, until one day the baggage train bringing the pay chest was ambushed and the pay chest was stolen. It has not pleased the men, as you can probably imagine. Add to that the fact that the local tribesmen keep nipping away at us both inside the forts and outside, and it is all leading to a mounting tension across the three forts. The men are starting to resent being sent out on patrols. I don't like to say it, but there is a very real risk of open mutiny." Jovian glanced away as if the very notion of a mutiny offended him, and he was ashamed.

"Truly, morale is that bad?" asked Corvo.

"The worst I've ever witnessed in my long career, that's for sure. True, the centurions and optios and some of the old sweats remain steadfast, but whether that will be enough to hold things together remains to be seen. Losing the pay chest was the last straw even for some of the steadier men. It doesn't help that we're spread so thin across the three forts this side of the Rhenus. There just aren't enough of us to man the forts and carry out regular patrols, especially with the steady stream of casualties we're enduring. Most of the legion is based in the larger forts on the other side of the Rhenus."

"Why doesn't my father send for more men?" asked Crispus.

"As far as I know he has, but they either won't or can't come," replied Jovian.

"Won't?" probed Corvo.

"You'd have to ask the legate about that." Jovian was reluctant to say more in front of the son of his commanding officer.

"You can speak freely in our company, Jovian," Corvo prompted.

Jovian looked at Arus. He knew the man's reputation as a spymaster and fixer for the legate and was clearly unsure whether he could truly trust him.

"It's fine, Centurion. I'm off duty," said Arus, smiling.

Jovian nodded, though he was uncertain that men like Arus were ever off duty. "The official line being given for the absence of reinforcements from the other side of the Rhenus is that with the imminent onset of winter, they must remain there until the spring and the new campaigning season, as they do every year in peacetime."

"And unofficially?" asked Corvo.

"Unofficially they say that Tribune Helvius, the legate's second-in-command, has been forbidden to send reinforcements."

"By whom?" asked Crispus.

"Either Legate Scipio or the emperor."

"Scipio is here?" asked Arus.

"Yes, he commands the Twentieth, who are also based on the other side of the Rhenus to the north-west. In all likelihood, he has probably also taken command of the Twenty-Second on that side of the river."

"But they are my father's men. He has no right to do that," spat Crispus bitterly.

"It all stinks of a conspiracy to make your father fail," said Arus, looking at Crispus. "Send him across the Rhenus to put down a rebellion which Jovian here says didn't even exist but probably does now due to his actions, and then deny him the men to successfully accomplish his mission. His inevitable failure will give the emperor the excuse he needs to remove another piece from the board that he perceives as a threat."

"But my father is innocent. He has always been a loyal servant of the Empire," said Crispus.

"He has, but when enough poison is drip-fed into somebody's ear, it eventually sticks. There are other forces at play here behind the emperor. What about the Eagle?" said Arus, turning to face Jovian again. "Tell me that wasn't lost too when the pay chest was stolen?"

"No, for once Fortune smiled on us. The standard-bearer is bedridden with some malady back in one of the big forts on the other side of the Rhenus, and neither he nor the Eagle travelled with the pay chest. The escort wasn't anywhere near large enough and as far as we know, all bar one of them was slaughtered, not that we've found any trace of the baggage train."

"All bar one?" inquired Corvo.

"One man made it to here and told us what happened. He said that a couple of the men tried to hide the pay chest just before the ambush started; he didn't know if they succeeded. He died shortly afterwards, before he could tell us where the ambush took place."

"So there could be some more survivors?" asked Arus.

"There could be, but I hope for their sake that there aren't. What these barbarians do to the men they capture…" Jovian let the words hang in the air, though everyone knew what he meant.

"Why did my father request such a small escort for the baggage train?" asked Crispus. "It doesn't sound like him to be so … negligent."

"He didn't. Legate Scipio organised it. Your father had no say and was furious when the survivor told us just how few men had been guarding it," explained Jovian.

"A sceptic might suggest that Scipio wanted the baggage train to be ambushed, knowing that it would reflect badly on your father," said Arus.

"And it would only be my father's men affected, as the money for the soldiers on the other side of the Rhenus would have already been withdrawn," added Crispus.

"What was the purpose of your patrol today?" Corvo asked Jovian.

"The legate is keen for us to keep sending out patrols in the hope of locating the ambush site and maybe finding the pay chest. He also wants to show the locals that we're not intimidated by them, but in truth all these patrols are doing is thinning our numbers, eroding our morale and provoking the locals." Jovian's face started to colour as he realised that he had probably overstepped by criticising his commanding officer's orders. "Begging your pardon, sir. I have the greatest of admiration for your father and believe he's been well and truly shafted. But while I will always carry out his orders, I do find myself questioning the wisdom of some of them."

"It's all right, Centurion. You've done nothing wrong," replied Crispus. "I appreciate and respect your honesty. If more followed your example, the Empire would be a better place for it."

"Well, it's been a long day. I suggest we retire and see what tomorrow brings once we reach Fort Felix. In the meantime, Centurion Jovian, I am instructing you to cease all patrols outside these walls unless specific new information as to the whereabouts of our missing men or the pay chest comes to light, in which case you are to immediately send a messenger to Fort Felix," ordered Arus.

"With all due respect, sir, the legate…"

"The legate will be fine, Centurion. I will explain when I see him tomorrow. You just concentrate on holding things here together, eh?"

"I'll do my best, sir. Thank you. Right, I'd best be off to carry out my rounds." Jovian got to his feet and listened to the howling wind and driving rain. "The winters here kill more of us than those hairy-backed barbarians ever do." He pulled his cloak about him, straightened his helmet and opened the door to the outside world. A cold blast rushed past him, making Arus shiver. "Good night," he said, and then he was gone.

CHAPTER 3

Despite the driving rain and the howling wind, Corvo and his fellow officers all slept well, the exhaustion of their recent journey finally catching up with them. After a plain but generous helping of bread and cheese washed down by watered wine, Corvo and his men marched out of Fort Duma under the watchful gaze of its surly garrison. Jovian had told Corvo that Fort Felix, where Legate Crispus was based, was approximately half a day's march to the west and to help them get there, he had assigned a jovial legionary by the name of Gemmellus.

They had been marching for a little over an hour when Gemmellus gave the signal to halt, before quietly crouching down and gesturing for everyone to do likewise. Corvo had then slowly and quietly made his way up the line to where Gemmellus was staring off into the trees to their east.

"Trouble?" whispered Corvo.

Gemmellus didn't reply. Instead, he carefully pulled a large fern leaf aside and pointed at something in the distance. Corvo peered in that direction but was initially unable to see what had drawn the other man's attention. However, as his eyes started to acclimatise to the gloomy interior of that part of the forest, he began to see a number of shapes standing stock-still, as if they were listening to something. Eventually, they moved off towards the north. As they went, Corvo was alarmed to discover that there were actually a lot more of them than his eyes had been able to discern. He turned to Gemmellus and raised his eyebrows.

"They send patrols out too," he said by way of explanation. "They're usually larger than ours, so we do our best to avoid them. That was one of the larger ones. I suspect news of your arrival has reached their chieftain and he's curious to find out who you are."

"Well, he's going to have to wait his turn. Well done, Legionary Gemmellus, I'm not sure that I would have spotted them. You've earned your pay today."

"If only there was something to pay me with, eh, Centurion?"

Despite himself, Corvo chuckled. He patted the man on the shoulder and the soldier beamed in response. "Lead on, Legionary Gemmellus."

Gemmellus got to his feet and quietly resumed their journey west. Corvo hung back for a moment as he waited for Flavius. "Tell the men to keep quiet, Lucius. There is a large enemy patrol to our north, seemingly out hunting us. If it hadn't been for Gemmellus, I think we might have blundered straight into them. Pass it down the line."

Flavius nodded, then turned and whispered to the man behind him, who happened to be Centurion Galba. He in turn passed the news to the man behind him, until eventually everyone in the column was aware and was on heightened alert.

By mid-afternoon, the trees had begun to thin. The rain had also finally stopped, and the weak winter sun now filtered through gaps in the canopy of leaves above, bathing the men in pale light and bringing some welcome relief from the oppressive gloom of the forest. A short while later they arrived at a small clearing. At the centre of this clearing sat another wooden fort almost identical in size and structure to Fort Duma. It had been built in one of the rare natural clearings found in the dense forests of Germania, but the ground around it had also been cleared for some distance in every direction. If an enemy were to attack the fort, the defenders would have at least some chance of spotting them and raising the alarm before they were at their gates.

"Fort Felix, I take it?" said Corvo, sidling alongside Gemmellus, who had once again hunkered down just inside the treeline out of sight of anyone who might be watching, including the fort's sentries.

"It is," replied Gemmellus.

"Then let's go. I am eager to see the legate." Corvo made to stand, but Gemmellus grasped his forearm and held it with enough pressure to stop him from standing. "What is it?"

"I'm not sure yet," replied Gemmellus. "Do you hear that?"

Corvo removed his helmet and listened for a few moments. "I don't hear anything."

"Exactly. No rustling of leaves, no birdsong, nothing."

"All the activity in and around the fort has probably scared the wildlife off — that or they've hunted it to extinction."

"Not the birds," replied Gemmellus.

"Well, perhaps our arrival has scared them away."

"No, that's not it." Gemmellus turned his gaze from the distant fort and began to scan the treeline to the north and west of the fort. After a little while, just as Corvo was about to tell him it was time they moved on, Gemmellus grunted in satisfaction when his patience finally paid off. "There!" He pointed to the northern treeline, and once again Corvo failed to see what had piqued his interest, but then a flicker of movement caught his eye. From that distance Corvo couldn't be sure what he had seen, but there had definitely been something there.

"I saw something, but I couldn't tell you what it was."

"A warrior. And he won't be alone."

"The same ones we saw earlier?" asked Corvo, his hand instinctively travelling towards the pommel of his gladius.

"I don't know. It seems unlikely. They were heading north, not west. I'm going to go and take a closer look. I recommend you all stay here and await my return. If I'm not back within two hundred breaths, I suggest you make your own way to the fort without me, as my head will probably have been taken as an ornament for some hairy bastard's tent pole. Just be careful when approaching the fort, though, as the men are likely to be nervous about intruders. They may well shoot arrows first and ask questions later."

"Good advice, Legionary Gemmellus. Do you want company?"

"I'm better on my own, Centurion. You and your men make more noise than a brothel on pay day. No offence."

Corvo grinned. "None taken."

"I'll be back shortly," said Gemmellus. He quickly melted into the trees behind them.

Corvo watched him go and then turned his attention to the treeline, where he thought he'd seen someone earlier.

"Company?" asked Flavius as he came and crouched beside his friend.

"The lack of bird noise made Gemmellus suspicious that we were not alone, and sure enough he claimed to have seen someone over there."

"Tribesmen?"

"Probably."

"Did you see anything?"

"I saw something, though what it was I couldn't tell you. However, after this morning's narrow escape, I've come to trust Gemmellus' instincts and judgement."

"Where is he, Marcus?" asked Flavius, glancing around.

"He's gone for a closer look."

"On his own?" asked Flavius, alarmed.

"We all make too much noise, apparently."

"Ah, he must have been talking about you, because I'm as quiet as a lamb," Flavius replied with a smile.

"A lamb being led to slaughter, perhaps," said Corvo, slowly shaking his head. He turned back to face the treeline. If there was someone there now, they were staying well concealed within the trees. He stared for some time but could make nothing out in the gloom.

A muffled sound from behind startled Corvo, and he had just begun to turn to investigate when Gemmellus suddenly appeared at his side.

"Another scouting party, different to the one we saw earlier, maybe ten strong. They've obviously been watching the fort for some time, judging by the depth of their imprints and the flattened foliage." Corvo was impressed Gemmellus could tell all of that just by looking at the ground but didn't want to show his own ignorance of such matters, so kept quiet. "They've gone now."

"In which direction?"

"North. Back to their camp with the other lot we saw this morning, I should think. They've undoubtedly left a couple of lookouts somewhere, though I couldn't locate them. Now would be a good time to cross to the fort, though what I said about not startling the sentries still stands."

"Very well. Get them quietly to their feet, Lucius, just in case the tribesmen have a change of heart and decide to double-back. Lead on, Legionary Gemmellus," said Corvo.

The men were soon on their feet and after a quick glance left and right, Gemmellus led the men out of the treeline and across the clearing towards Fort Felix. Their sudden appearance had already been noted. Although he couldn't make out what was being said, Corvo could hear orders being barked out by centurions and optios, and he grinned to himself as he imagined scores of legionaries rushing to put their armour and helmets on as they climbed the steps to the ramparts. As they drew nearer to the gates, Corvo also realised that Gemmellus' warning about cautiously approaching the fort had been justified. The fort's ramparts were now crammed with men armed with javelins, and he saw perhaps a score of bowmen with arrows nocked and pointing their way.

Corvo brought the column to a halt one hundred paces from the fort's gates, and then together with Arus, advanced to within thirty paces before coming to a stop. Leaving the men stranded in a clearing with their backs to the forest made Corvo nervous; he prayed that Gemmellus was right, and the tribesmen had left the area and hadn't returned in force. He also hoped that some of the men on the ramparts had been tasked with keeping a watchful eye on the surrounding treelines, not just he and his men.

"That's far enough. Announce yourselves," said the optio from the rampart above the fort's gates. Corvo and Arus exchanged a look as they recalled receiving exactly the same challenge when they had shown up outside Fort Lipa in Armenia. Back then they had been dressed in local Armenian clothes, and the sentries had had every right to be cautious. This time Corvo, Arus and most of their men were in Roman uniforms, although the gladiators continued to wear outfits of their choosing.

"Do you want to try again, or would you prefer it if I tried this time, given what happened in Armenia?" Corvo asked Arus wryly.

"No, I'll try. I've got to be lucky sooner or later," replied Arus.

"Come on, speak up. I haven't got all day!" shouted the optio.

"Impatient little fellow, isn't he?" Arus whispered to Corvo. "I am Cornelius Arus, on Legate Crispus' staff, and this is Centurion Marcus Ovidius Corvo and his men. We are here to see the legate, if you'd be so kind as to tell him we're here."

"I don't recognise you from the legate's staff," replied the optio.

"That is probably because I have been away running errands for the legate. Now, I'm tired and thirsty and just a little nervous about the fact that a horde of tribesmen could come hurtling out of those trees and catch us in the open, so would you please be so good as to fetch the legate? And quickly."

"The legate doesn't like being disturbed. He's very particular about that."

"Just fetch him, you imbecile!" Arus bellowed so loudly that Corvo flinched. He also worried that any passing tribesmen might be tempted to come and investigate, and he cast nervous glances around the treeline.

The optio didn't reply and instead disappeared from view. Corvo imagined the man was hurrying down the steps and across the square to wherever the legate was holed up, all the while trying to drum up the courage to disturb the legate. A few moments later, the optio returned and an older man in the uniform of a legate appeared on the rampart next to him. The man had aged considerably in the eighteen months since Corvo had last seen him. However, there was no doubt that this slightly hunched figure was Legate Publius Crispus, the man responsible for sending Corvo on the mission to Armenia and in whose hands the futures of his men rested.

Legate Crispus grabbed the wooden palisade and leant forward for a better look. "By the gods, is that you, Cornelius?" Although his body appeared weaker and frail, his voice was strong and confident.

"It is, Legate."

"You're alive?"

"Despite the best efforts of many men, yes, I am."

"I never thought to see you again."

"There were indeed times when I doubted you would, Legate, yet here I am. What is more, I have somebody who is very much looking forward to seeing you." Arus beamed as he spoke.

The look on the legate's face, however, suggested that his mind had not yet quite caught up with reality. It was only when his son stepped forward from the cluster of men behind Arus and removed his helmet, that the truth dawned.

"Gaius?"

"Father!" called the young man, smiling widely.

The legate's legs seemed to buckle slightly, and he held on to the palisade more tightly. "Well, don't just stand there! Open the gates, you fools!" he shouted. Below him, the beam holding the double gates closed was lifted clear by four legionaries, while two others swung the gates open.

In the distance a wolf howled, its pitiful call soon answered by another and then a third.

"I suggest you all get in on the double, Cornelius, as some wolves have two legs and carry spears," called the legate before turning and heading down the steps.

"Company, forward at the double," ordered Corvo, and soon everyone was inside the fort and the gates were barred once again.

Another howl pierced the air, closer this time. Corvo was no longer convinced that it was a wolf and was suddenly very glad to be inside the fort's walls, though he couldn't shake the feeling that rather than being safe, he was in fact trapped.

After embracing his son and then his old friend Arus, the legate issued orders that Corvo and his men be taken to the galley and fed, while others were set the task of arranging accommodation for all of them. Then he disappeared to his quarters to speak with his son. It was not until early evening that the legate finally sent for Arus and Corvo, both of whom by then had eaten, washed and rested.

Arus knocked on the wooden door of the legate's command room. After a brusque, "Come," he pushed open the door and stepped in, followed by Corvo. The legate was sitting behind a small wooden table that appeared to be covered with a large open map, held flat and in place by a half dozen stones. The legate's son sat on the opposite side of the table, now washed and dressed in a fresh uniform. Corvo marvelled at how much better he looked, no longer the emaciated waif they had rescued from the Armenian prison several months earlier.

"Welcome, Cornelius, Centurion. Please come and take a seat," said the legate, beaming. He too looked a different man to the one they had first seen, but unlike his son, his transformation had taken mere hours. "Wine?" Both Arus and Corvo nodded. The legate poured them a generous helping each and indicated the seats next to his son. When everyone was seated and holding a drink, the legate raised his cup. "Your good health, men." When he had taken a couple of mouthfuls, he set his cup down and observed the three men opposite him. "I never thought this day would come. You actually did it. To steal my son and those other men from under the Armenians' noses — and deep behind their own lines, no less — I never truly thought it possible."

"Yet here we are," replied Arus with a grin.

"Yet here you are. I can never truly repay you, either of you. What price can you put on the life of your only son? None. I can't even stand on the forum in Rome and shout about your heroics." The legate's gaze dropped, as if he were deep in thought.

"How is it you find yourself here, Legate?" asked Arus.

The legate looked up. "It seems our beloved emperor has grown jealous of my successes, minor though they are, and wanted me far from Rome and the public eye. Who knows, perhaps he even saw me as a threat, ridiculous as that sounds. The few friends I still retain in the eternal city — not that they would ever admit to being such in the company of strangers — tell me he grows ever more paranoid, seeing enemies where there are none. Men like me. As a consequence, I was stripped of my beloved Eleventh Legion and sent here to quell a rebellion that I don't think ever existed."

"It didn't exist?" queried Arus. He and Corvo exchanged a glance, remembering what Jovian had told them.

"No, though I think our patrols and reoccupation of these forts have likely stoked one now. Who knows, perhaps that was the emperor's intent all along. I would have thought he's busy enough dealing with the Parthians in Armenia, though you of course would know that better than me. And what did they give me to put down this alleged rebellion? The Twenty-Second, that's what. A legion that has hardly covered itself in glory in the past, and a handful of Gaulish cavalry." The legate took another mouthful of wine. "And most of the legion are stationed in the forts on the other side of the Rhenus, leaving me with two cohorts spread across three forts on this side of the river."

"Centurion Vitus Jovian at Fort Duma told us that the tribesmen just keep probing all the forts, but haven't as yet launched an all-out attack on any one of them," said Corvo.

"Jovian — he's a good man. He fares well?"

Corvo nodded. "Despite enduring another attack while out on patrol and losing some more of his men, he is in remarkably good spirits."

"Yes, Gaius told me about that. Lucky your company happened to be close by or it could have ended very differently. Something else I am indebted to you for, Centurion. And yes, Jovian is right — they haven't launched a major attack on one of the forts, thank Jupiter, but then they don't really need to, as they just keep chipping away at our patrols and thinning out our numbers before melting back into these damn forests."

"Then why keep sending these patrols out?" asked Arus.

"Because I have to try and find the pay chest. The baggage train was ambushed."

"Yes, Jovian told us that too. One man made it back but was unable to tell you where the ambush took place before he succumbed to his injuries," added Corvo.

"Quite. And as I'm sure you can imagine, the men are not happy. Some of my officers even warn me that we could be facing a rebellion in our own ranks, never mind from the tribesmen. Not that I trust many of them — they're not my men, you understand. A few of the officers are with me, men like Jovian, but is it enough to hold the men together? The loss of the pay chest has played right into the emperor's hands. His decision to exile me to this backwater, for that is what it is, exile, is now vindicated. If I am not able to retrieve the pay chest and restore morale to these men under my command, my life expectancy can probably be measured in weeks or perhaps even days. I will die either at the hands of an assassin sent by the emperor or at the hands of my own men. I don't need to tell you that soldiers only follow a successful general, and then only if they are being paid or have access to regular plunder. Here I have been neither successful nor able to reward them. So you see my dilemma?"

Arus and Corvo both nodded.

"Why don't you summon the cohorts from across the river and flood the forest to try and find the ambush site?" asked Tribune Crispus.

"I have, but I keep being given excuses by Tribune Helvius as to why he can't send them, none of which are valid. I'm no fool — I know that it's not his doing and it's that bastard Scipio pulling the strings, no doubt on the emperor's command. Not that he would have needed much convincing — there's always been animosity between the two of us, as I'm sure you recall, Cornelius?" Arus nodded. "The tribesmen know we are weak and may even know about the dissent. If they learn that there is no chance of us receiving reinforcements, they may well launch a full scale attack on these three forts — I would, if I were in their position. Moreover, we are heading into winter, and winters in this land are brutal. The campaigning season is over, and the men across the river would rather see the winter out in the large garrisons they now occupy than in some wooden hovel like this." The legate was clearly struggling to maintain a brave face. "Anyway, these are all my problems, not yours. You have both done far more than I expected or had any right to ask. You have returned my son safely and for that you have my undying gratitude. More importantly, I suspect, for your men at least, I have these." The legate reached under his desk, lifted up a plain wooden box and placed it on the table in front of him. "Some time ago now, I had my clerk draw up manumission papers and pardons. None of them bear names or are dated because … well, truthfully I didn't expect to see any of you again."

"Then why go to the effort of having them drawn up, Legate?" asked Corvo.

"Because a man must always have hope. Without hope, there is no point in living. Now, I suggest that in the morning we have a parade, and you can present these to your men. They are then free to follow their own paths. Any regular soldiers will have the opportunity to either be returned to their original unit or transfer here, under my command. They will receive a cash bonus as and when I locate the pay chest. I hope your men are prepared to be patient?"

"Thank you, Legate," said Corvo. "I will advise them of the situation and ask for their patience."

"As for you, Centurion, I don't know what to offer. Ordinarily I would have used my connections to secure you a posting wherever you chose to serve, but I regret that those days are gone … for now, at least. Any words in support of you would now, I fear, be seen as dripping in poison rather than honey, and you are better off without them. You too are welcome to remain here — you all are. Jupiter knows I could use your help, but you've all gone above and beyond your duty to me and to Rome, and you should be allowed to choose your own destiny from this point on. It's the least I can do."

"One thing, Legate. Does the emperor know about our mission to Armenia?" asked Arus.

"Not from my lips he doesn't, but truthfully, I don't know. However, he has spies everywhere, and I suspect that is the case. Absences will have been noticed, yours in particular. No Roman general is allowed his own personal force, which is just another reason why I think my days may be numbered. His spies will no doubt have told him I am building an army with which to overthrow him."

The mood turned morose as the men took in what they had been told.

"One more drink, and then I will retire. I think we would all benefit from an early night," said the legate. He poured himself another measure and then began to refill the others as they all leant forward, proffering their cups. When they were all filled, the legate and his son stood but signalled for Arus and Corvo to remain seated. This toast was in their honour. "To good officers, good friends and brave men. I salute you." The legate had just started to raise the cup to his lips when a sharp rap on the wooden door startled them all. "Come!"

The door opened immediately, and a young, nervous-looking tribune stepped in. When he saw that the legate was not alone, he seemed to blanche.

"Yes, what is it, Ortius?" the legate demanded. The young tribune went to speak but glanced at Arus, Tribune Crispus and Corvo, clearly unsure whether he should impart his news in the presence of these strangers. "Come on, man, spit it out. Whatever you've got to say, you can say in front of these men."

Ortius nodded slightly, as if coming to the same conclusion, or perhaps he was just trying to fortify himself for the task ahead. "Sorry to disturb you, Legate, but we have trouble."

"Tribesmen? Are we under attack?" asked the legate. Corvo was already getting to his feet.

"No, sir." Ortius glanced at Arus and Corvo again.

"Well?" the legate prompted, his patience seemingly having run its course.

"There's been a fight in the mess hall, sir, between our men and the newcomers. One man is dead."

Corvo and Arus exchanged a nervous look. Their early night was going to have to wait.

CHAPTER 4

After grabbing their sword belts and helmets, the officers hurried over to the mess hall, Ortius following in their wake. The noise coming from the hall as they approached it was tumultuous, and the officers glanced at one another as they gathered outside its doors. After checking everyone was ready, the legate barged through the doors, trying to exude as much authority as possible. It was so noisy, and the majority of the hall's occupants were so preoccupied, that only a few noticed the officers' arrival and quietened down. The rest continued to hurl insults and furniture at one another. It was a scene of devastation and disorder. The mess hall wasn't very large, as the garrison size didn't warrant it, and it therefore didn't take very many men to make it look crammed, especially when all its occupants were on their feet. Tonight, it was full almost to capacity.

"Silence!" bellowed the legate. Those closest to him glanced his way and most began to quieten down. Others, whether because they didn't hear him or didn't care, continued to shout and threaten, but the fighting had at least ceased. "I said silence!" This time most of the room fell quiet, the legate's voice booming off the walls. The legate stared menacingly at the men until he had absolute silence.

Meanwhile, Corvo, who had been standing quietly to the legate's right, had also been appraising the situation. On one side of the hall stood some of his men, many of whom were bleeding from their mouths and noses. On the other side of the hall, looking equally bloody, stood a number of the fort's garrison. Standing between them and acting as a buffer despite being outnumbered by both parties was Atilus, some gladiators and a couple of regular legionaries under Corvo's command. He and his small band were doing their best to keep the two warring factions apart and had clearly been the reason the fighting had stopped. Outnumbered they may have been, but intimidated they most certainly were not, and it was clear that neither party fancied tangling with Atilus and his men. On the floor close to Atilus' feet was a body, though Corvo couldn't identify who it was as they were lying face down.

Corvo looked over at his men that had taken part in the brawl and was not surprised to see that front and centre was Traianus. The men standing behind him were all his former comrades. Corvo smiled at the inevitability of it all. He had recruited Traianus, a former centurion, and more than a score of his former comrades, from a penal quarry outside Rome, to accompany him on his mission to rescue Tribune Crispus. Traianus and his men had been sent to the quarry for refusing to press home an attack and rescue some beleaguered troops from another cohort. As a consequence, those men had been slaughtered. Traianus' senior officers had been executed or sent into exile, where they had later succumbed to an imperial assassin, but Traianus and the other low-level ringleaders had just received a severe flogging and been sent to penal colonies. For the comrades of the men who had been left to die, it had not been enough; in their eyes, justice had not been served.

"What in Hades is going on here?" demanded the legate. Nobody answered, but a few men — especially those from the fort's garrison — had the good sense to at least cast their gazes down. "Well?" Still nobody answered. "You, Batilus," said the legate, pointing at a stockily built man in his early forties standing in front of the garrison men, "tell me now what happened, or I'll have the skin off your back." A loud, ugly murmuring rippled through the ranks of the garrison men. "You're no stranger to the lash, Batilus, so I suggest you're quick about it."

"Why don't you ask those bastards?" replied the legionary, spitting on the floor.

"You insolent dog!" shouted Ortius. "How dare you speak to your commanding officer in that fashion? I'll have…"

"It's all right, Tribune. I'll handle this," said the legate, putting a hand on Ortius' shoulder. "Explain yourself, Batilus, and be quick about it."

Batilus' posture was still defensive, but his tone when he addressed his commanding officer this time was at least more conciliatory. "These bastards are the cowards who refused to come to the aid of our brothers in Dacia. They just stood there and watched as our men were butchered." The men behind him shouted their agreement. The air was heavy with anger and hate.

"They were dead whether we attacked or not. No sense in more good men dying for nothing!" shouted Traianus in response. His own men now shouted their agreement, and the hall once again erupted into a cacophony of noise.

"Good men? There isn't a good man among you. None of you were fit to kiss the feet of the men that died that day. Cowards!" The two sides surged towards each other and began to kick and throw punches, while Atilus and his handful of men tried desperately to keep them apart, not holding back against either party. While the two sides were separated once again with the help of Optio Nerva, who had arrived with a squad of guards from Corvo's detachment, Corvo closed his eyes and winced. When Centurion Jovian at Fort Duma had mentioned the Twenty-Second Legion, it had pricked a memory deep within Corvo's mind, but he had been unable to fully recall it. Then, when the legate had bemoaned the fact he had been saddled with the Twenty-Second, it had again troubled him. Now it all made sense. Out of all the legions, they had had to run into Traianus' old legion, one where bad blood ran deep and memories were long. Had Jovian recognised them? Was that why he had insisted that Corvo's men be bunked separately, away from his own men? If so, he had demonstrated great sense and foresight.

"Centurion … Centurion?"

Corvo turned to face the legate. Evidently he was waiting for an answer, but Corvo had been too lost in thought to hear the question. The legate did not seem amused.

"Apologies, Legate. What did you ask me?"

"I asked you if this was true, what Batilus has just said."

"I was not there, Legate, so I cannot say with any certainty." Thinking Corvo was going to defend his men and call he and his comrades liars, Batilus and his supporters began to grumble and raise their voices in protest. "But," said Corvo, raising his own voice, "that is certainly how I heard events played out, and others in my command have corroborated it too."

"And you didn't think it wise to warn me that you were bringing such dishonourable men into my fort, to live and work among the friends and comrades of those they betrayed and let down?"

"Apologies, Legate. I did not make the connection until just now."

"Neither did I, Legate," added Arus, seeking to cool the legate's rising temper. "The centurion could not afford to be overly selective when forming his company for the mission you entrusted him with."

The tension seemed to seep out of the legate's shoulders. "No, no, of course not. Just bad luck … something that has dogged me ever since I arrived here, it seems. You were fortunate that none of the Twenty-Second recognised you when you camped at Fort Duma the other night."

"Actually, there was a deal of discontent — not to this extreme," said Arus, indicating the body, "but the garrison seemed unhappy. We thought it was because Centurion Jovian had ordered the men to move barracks and make way for our men, but perhaps there was more to it after all."

"Centurion Jovian is an astute man who should have risen higher in the ranks. It would not have surprised me if he recognised these men and sought to segregate them to avert trouble," said the legate, nodding. "Who is the dead man?" he asked, turning to face his men.

"Legionary Artorius, sir," replied Batilus. "One of those dogs stabbed him in the back. They can't face a man head-on." The men behind Batilus roared their agreement, but their mocking was soon rivalled by a renewed tide of threats from Traianus and his men.

"Let you and me settle this now, and we'll see who the coward is, you fat…" Traianus' words were cut off by another roar from the legate.

"Silence! The next man who speaks without permission will find himself on latrine duty until he drops dead." The legate stared at both leaders until they both lost their nerve and looked away. The legate's gaze then settled on Traianus. "You, what is your name?"

"Traianus," Traianus replied. The legate stared at him intently and raised an eyebrow. "Traianus … sir."

"Better. Did you kill Artorius?"

"No … sir."

"Did you see who did?"

"No, sir."

"He's lying!" shouted somebody behind Batilus, but by the time the legate turned in their direction, the perpetrator had melted into the crowd and his comrades weren't about to give him up.

"Can any one of you say with certainty who killed Artorius?" asked the legate, turning again to face his own men. "Well?"

"Does it matter? One of ours is dead, so one of theirs should die," said Batilus sourly.

"And die they would, if one of you … anyone … could point to a man and state that he was the killer. But you can't, and I am not about to execute a random man. By the gods, there has to be something that separates us from those tree-dwelling barbarians outside our walls. We cannot sink to their level. I will not permit it."

"You can't let them get away with murder, Legate," said Batilus pleadingly.

"Are you now telling me what I can and can't do in my own fort, Legionary Batilus?"

"No, sir!"

"That is wise. Since nobody will own up to the murder and none of you can point the murderer out to me, I have no choice but to punish Traianus and all of his men. I trust you are in agreement, Centurion?" said the legate, turning to look at Corvo.

"I consider you have no other option, Legate."

"Not unless they all want to be flogged, and like Batilus here, I'm guessing they too are no strangers to the lash."

"So once more, they are to evade justice," said Batilus bitterly.

"Enough!" roared the legate. "I am tired of you challenging my every word and decision, Batilus. One more utterance from you and you will endure the same fate as these men. I have told you they will be collectively punished, and they will be. That is all you need to concern yourself with. You are Roman soldiers, poor examples of them, I grant you, but Roman soldiers nonetheless. Let Jupiter be my witness: you will be transformed into useful members of the emperor's legions once again or you will be ground into dust. Do I make myself clear?" A few men mumbled their assent while others just nodded. "Your commanding officer just asked you a question — give me an answer."

This time, both sets of men roared, "Yes!" But Corvo could tell their enthusiasm wasn't genuine, especially with his men. There was still a great deal of bad blood, and it would need to be resolved one way or another.

"And what is to be the punishment for these men, Legate?" said Arus, stepping alongside the legate in a show of support.

The legate stroked his chin. "I think they…" The legate never got to finish his sentence, as the doors to the mess hall burst open and everyone turned to look at the red-faced legionary carrying a torch.

"What?" demanded the legate irritably.

Seemingly overawed, the young legionary could not find his tongue.

"Do you have something to report, son?" asked Arus, not unkindly. The legionary nodded. "Then just look at the legate and tell him. Ignore everybody else."

The young legionary did as bid and turned to face the legate, snapping to attention and offering a smart salute. He was trying desperately to pretend that nobody else was listening to him, and when he spoke there was a nervous crack in his voice.

"Beg to report, sir, but there is shouting outside."

"What? Tribesmen? Are we under attack?"

"Not when I left, sir. We can hear tribesmen and what sounded like Roman voices. It's too dark to see much, sir, but we think someone is being chased."

"Centurion Corvo, your men are to stay here under your command. Tribune Ortius, get our men to the ramparts, now!"

Corvo was going to argue, but thought better of it and watched with disappointment as the legate, Ortius and the men with Batilus raced out of the mess hall, grabbing their weapons and helmets, which were stacked against the far wall, as they went. When it was just Corvo and his men left behind, Corvo turned to Atilus.

"Follow them, find out what's happening and report back."

The former gladiator nodded, grabbed his gladius and hurried out of the hall towards the ramparts. Arus smiled when he saw the look on Corvo's face.

"For the love of the gods, go, Corvo, before your countenance sours the wine and rots our food."

"But the legate…"

"The legate will be fine. If he says anything just tell him I sent you up there."

Corvo didn't need to be told again. He turned on his heel and raced out of the hall. He was soon on the ramparts to the left of the gate. To his right was the legate, Tribune Crispus and Tribune Ortius. To his left stood Atilus.

"Centurion Corvo, I thought I ordered you to remain with your men?" said the legate, without turning to face him.

"You did, Legate, but Arus told me I would be of more use to you here than down in the mess hall and sent me away."

"I see." The legate's attention was fixed on something in the gloom and Corvo followed his gaze.

"There," said Tribune Ortius, and he pointed to where a few pinpricks of light danced towards the edge of the forest. A few moments later they could all make out the guttural sound of a number of tribesmen as they emerged from the trees, carrying torches. Their voices were animated and although Corvo couldn't understand a word they were saying, he nevertheless got their meaning. They were hunting someone.

Just then, the sound of a man running at speed towards them could be made out and the Romans leant forward with their own torches, trying to illuminate the ground in front of the fort. The man was shouting in heavily accented Latin for the gates to be opened, but they could not yet see him.

"Legate?" asked the tribune.

"I'm not opening the gates for one man. There could be a horde of barbarians waiting in the dark for me to do just that, and by the morning all of our heads will be decorating tent poles throughout the forest. Archers stand ready."

Along the northern rampart a dozen men nocked arrows.

The man was now screaming as he raced towards the fort.

"There!" shouted Corvo, but even as he pointed, they watched the man's body jerk as first one and then another arrow struck him squarely in the back. The man collapsed to the ground but desperately tried to crawl forward towards the gates. Out of the gloom strode a grinning tribesman. He stopped behind the soldier and pulled his head back by his blond hair. Then, after grinning up at the fort ramparts, he ran his sword across the wounded man's throat.

"Take that bastard down!" shouted the legate. Half a dozen arrows were immediately released, four of them striking home. The warrior collapsed, already dead before his face smacked into the wet mud of the track leading to the fort.

More shouts drew their attention and from the northwest another man emerged from the dark, sprinting towards the fort and screaming for the gates to be opened. Behind him came half a dozen warriors, howling and shouting, invigorated by the chase. The legate had seen enough, and ignoring his own words from a short while before, he shouted, "Get those gates open! Archers, bring them down."

The archers opened up. Four of the warriors immediately dropped to the ground, but two were going to close in on their target before the archers could fire again. One of the tribesmen, a young warrior whose beard was not yet full, had drawn close enough to his target to strike. But fortune was not on his side and as chance would have it, his quarry stumbled and fell just as the warrior's sword sliced through the air where he had been just moments before. Running at full pelt and off-balance when he swung his sword, the young warrior also stumbled and hit the ground next to the other man. The man being chased — who Corvo could now see was wearing the tattered uniform of an auxiliary unit, which explained the accented Latin — was holding a dagger. Quick as a flash, he climbed onto the stricken tribesman, pinning him down with a knee on his chest before repeatedly plunging his blade into the man's throat.

But he had forgotten the last warrior, a big man clad in heavy bearskins who had struggled to keep up with his younger comrade, and who was now almost upon him. It was only when the auxiliary's bloodlust had been sated that he heard the warnings being shouted from the ramparts and turned to confront this new threat.

Watching from the ramparts, Corvo could see that it was already too late. The older warrior was nearly upon the auxiliary and the dagger the soldier was carrying would be of little use against the two-headed war axe the other man was carrying. Two arrows suddenly struck the warrior, one in the shoulder and one in his thigh, while others, hastily released with little aim, flew past him and dangerously close to the auxiliary soldier. The warrior looked at the two arrows as if they were nothing more than a nuisance and briefly glared at the ramparts. Then, roaring his anger, he snapped off the one protruding from his shoulder, the thick bearskin having prevented the head from piercing too deeply.

While the tribesman was momentarily distracted, the auxiliary soldier tried to rise, but the warrior merely pushed him back down to the ground with his foot. Then he raised his axe high above his head, ready to deliver a powerful downward blow.

Corvo went to turn away, unable to bring himself to watch another good man be slaughtered, but as he did so, he caught a flash of movement to his left. Atilus had grabbed a pilum from a legionary standing next to him on the rampart and in one fluid movement, had released the javelin. It flew true and straight and was thrown with so much force that it went straight through the bearskin and the chainmail the warrior was wearing underneath and then into his heart. The warrior stood there for a few moments until the axe slipped from his grip, and then he collapsed backwards to the ground.

The legate and tribune both turned to see who had thrown the javelin, their gazes settling on the legionary who had been holding the pilum, but found he in turn was staring open-mouthed at Atilus.

Atilus, for his part, merely shrugged.

"Run, you fool!" shouted Batilus from further along the rampart, and everybody's attention returned to the fallen soldier. Recovering from the initial shock, he was now scrambling to his feet.

In the near distance, more torches were emerging from the trees. The auxiliary needed no further encouragement.

Summoning all his remaining strength, he sprinted for the gates, not stopping until he collapsed to the ground some strides within.

The moment he was inside, the legate bellowed for the gates to be closed. The tribesmen carrying the torches had continued to walk forward but stopped just outside of bow range. One of them, though, whether to demonstrate his bravery or just to defy the Roman defenders, walked another twenty paces forward. There he stopped, and after looking at his dead comrades scattered about him, he slowly turned his gaze towards the ramparts. He briefly studied the men manning the fort's walls, his eyes lingering on the legate.

"Archers, sir?" asked Tribune Ortius.

"Not yet."

The tribesman maintained his stare for a while longer and then hawked noisily and spat on the ground.

"That's a disgusting habit, and he's well and truly outstayed his welcome now. See him on his way, Tribune, if you please," said the legate. But by the time the order had been given, the tribesman had already turned and walked away, and the Roman arrows thudded harmlessly into the mud.

CHAPTER 5

The tribesmen faded back into the sanctuary of the trees, but their torches remained visible for some hours afterwards. Corvo wondered whether they were standing just out of sight, watching the fort and waiting for the Romans to lower their guard. Or perhaps the tribesmen had merely fixed the torches to the trees, to make the Romans think they were still there and to keep them on edge and tired. It was impossible to know without sending out scouts — a risk the legate could not afford to take. Therefore, half his men were ordered to stand-to on the ramparts while the other half rested uneasily in their barracks.

The desire for sleep had now deserted Corvo, and together with an equally anxious Flavius he instead found himself pacing up and down the fort's ramparts until the first rays of the winter sun appeared over the eastern horizon. The prospect of a day without rain did little to cheer him.

Corvo watched as a messenger hurried up the steps to the ramparts and after looking round, strode over to where Flavius was standing a few paces to Corvo's right, rubbing his hands together and stamping his feet in an attempt to keep warm. The night had been bitter, and the cold had seeped into their bones. Flavius nodded and dismissed the messenger and then came striding over to join Corvo.

"You have an officers' meeting just after the change of guard. Galba has the watch, and I am for my bunk."

Corvo nodded. Now that the likelihood of an enemy night attack had passed, he was feeling tired again and had been looking forward to getting his head down for a few hours, but it seemed that was going to have to wait.

"Good morning, men." Both men turned to see Arus smiling brightly at them. Neither of them had heard him approach — stealth was a necessary skill for anybody in his profession, no doubt, Corvo mused. Arus looked rested and alert, the complete opposite to the two of them. "Did I miss anything? I've slept like a Titan."

Corvo chose not to take the bait that was being offered. "No. They're not there. They tied their torches to the trees, knowing we'd have to stay alert all night to the possibility of attack while they went back to their women and beds."

"You've seen no one?" asked Arus, surprised.

"Not one. There are probably always a couple of men skulking around here, watching the fort, but no, the war band has definitely retreated."

"And you found it necessary to stay up and ensure that was the case?"

"We haven't been here a day yet and we've already antagonised the legate. I felt it was the least I could do by way of reparation."

"You weren't to know that Traianus and his men were going to kill a man."

"But that's just it — I should have known. Once I heard what legion was stationed in these forts, I should have remembered their history with that fool Traianus and anticipated trouble. But I didn't and now a man is dead, and we've done nothing but add to the legate's troubles."

"You are too hard on yourself, Centurion. Although an officer is always responsible for the men under his command, you cannot watch them all the time. There has to be trust. And as for the legate, he is not fragile and can look after himself."

"And how did that work out for Traianus' officers, after he and his men refused to attack? They probably didn't foresee that, but they paid for it with their lives."

"Oh, don't be so dramatic, Centurion. You are in no danger of suffering the same fate, if that is what troubles you. The legate is not that sort of man."

"I am not worried for myself, but for the good men around me, men like Lucius, Galba, Nerva, Atilus and others. I cannot allow their acts of bravery and glory to be tainted by the actions of one rotten apple."

"Nor will they be, I can assure you. Now, I wish to hear no more talk of this matter. Here comes the change of guard, so I think we have an officers' meeting to attend. Shall we?" Arus indicated that Corvo should lead the way. After one last glance towards the trees, Corvo headed down the steps and across the square to the building being used by the legate as his quarters.

Corvo and Arus were the last to arrive, with the legate, his son, Tribune Ortius and the Gaulish auxiliary who they had saved the night before, standing around the small wooden table in the middle of the room.

"Good morning, men," the legate greeted.

"Good morning, sir," replied Arus and Corvo, while exchanging nods of greeting with the other men.

"I have asked Vortrix to join us, as he has some information that I think you will find of interest." Corvo couldn't help but notice that the legate seemed energised, and more so than could be attributed to a good night's sleep. It made him wonder just how good this news was. "Now that everyone is here, Vortrix, perhaps you can tell these men exactly what you told me earlier."

"My name is Vortrix, and I am a duplicarius in the Gaulish cavalry attached to the Twenty-Second Legion. What is left of us has been barracked at Fort Otto, a half day's march to the northwest of here. Like the men stationed here and at Fort Duma, we have been ordered to carry out regular patrols, primarily to keep an eye on the tribesmen living in these woods, but also to try and find the location of the baggage train ambush. A week ago, we came across a small clearing which was unfamiliar to us and found the baggage train, or what was left of it. We had just dismounted and begun to search the site when we were surprised by a large war band of tribesmen. They had us surrounded — we had no choice but to try and fight our way out, but there were too many and eventually we had to surrender. Most of the men, including my decurion, were killed fighting, but six of us were taken prisoner. They…" It was obvious the man was loath to recall the memories, but knew that somehow he had to find the courage.

"It's all right, Duplicarius. Take your time," urged the legate, offering the man a cup of watered wine.

Vortrix gulped it down greedily and then wiped his mouth with the back of his hand. "Thank you, Legate. The men, they were cruelly tortured, me included." He lifted his tunic to reveal a crisscross pattern of livid scars and burn marks across his chest and back. "In the end, only Erdika — the man who was with me last night — and myself remained. The others had either been killed or had succumbed to their wounds. We knew that we wouldn't last more than another day. A messenger arrived at the tribesmen's camp yesterday, and there was a heated debate among their warriors — whatever news the messenger brought clearly agitated them. At the time we had no idea what that news was, but now I suspect you and your men had been spotted and the war band was sent out to find you. We thought they were going to kill us before they left.

Some were suggesting that — we didn't need to speak their words to understand that much — but their chieftain said no. Instead, he left us alive with just a handful of bored old warriors as guards before heading out with his war band to find you. We waited for them to drink themselves into a stupor while all the time working on our bonds. When we had freed our hands, it was just a matter of waiting for the right moment to make our escape. Everything went as we hoped, and after killing the guards we made a run for it. They had taken our horses, so we had to run as best we could through the forest. Poor Erdika was in worse shape than I and struggled to keep up, but I was not going to leave him. Just when I thought we were going to make it here, we ran into two of their young warriors, boys not yet old enough to shave. They were eager for the chance to prove themselves and claim their first kills, and I suppose they saw us as just that — weak and vulnerable. We were, but we were also determined. We killed the first boy with his own sword, but the second one turned tail and ran back the way they had come towards the war band. Then we just ran for all we were worth, but they were soon on our tracks. The rest you know."

"So now we know where both the ambush site and their camp is, but we don't have the men to launch a punitive action," said Corvo, confused. "I don't see how this necessarily helps us."

"Vortrix has missed out one salient detail in his account," said the legate with a smile. "Tell them what you saw there, Duplicarius."

"The pay chest from the baggage train."

"You're sure?" asked Arus.

"Perfectly. The chieftain showed it to his men before having it carried into his tent. If that isn't proof enough, I had to watch while his men forced coins down the throat of one of my comrades until he choked to death."

Nobody spoke for a moment, each no doubt silently visualising that scene inside their own head.

"We have to get it back," said Tribune Ortius matter-of-factly.

"We do, but as Centurion Corvo just said, we do not possess the men to attack their camp. We need the legion from the forts on the other side of the Rhenus," the legate's son replied.

"And they won't or can't come," said Arus.

"Not even now they know we've located the pay chest? Surely that would motivate them?"

"Let us not kid ourselves: I was sent here to fail, to give the emperor a reason to dispose of me, and failing I am," said the legate ruefully. "Tribune Helvius is a good man, but not an inspired one, and he commands very much by the book. As I have said before, he has no doubt been instructed by the emperor or one of his aides not to leave his forts under any circumstances, and he will remain there even if I command him to march out. He has no doubt been promised command of the Twenty-Second upon my demise. Loyalty has its limits."

"But he is guilty of disobeying an order from his commanding officer if he does not comply with your command," stated Tribune Ortius indignantly.

"Certainly, but if the emperor or Scipio, on behalf of the emperor, orders him to stay within the forts and he does not, he is guilty of committing treason."

"Then we are confounded," said the legate's son dismally.

"Not quite," said Corvo.

"You have a suggestion, Centurion?" asked the legate brightly.

"Perhaps."

"Well, don't be bashful. Share it with all of us."

"I will, but before I do so, I would like your permission to include Centurion Galba, Optio Flavius and Atilus in the meeting. I value all of their opinions highly."

"Atilus?"

"The man who threw the pilum and killed that big tribesman before he got a chance to chop our Gaulish friend here into many different pieces."

The legate nodded. "That was some throw. What rank does he hold?"

"He doesn't. He is a former gladiator who sought me out and asked to join our mission."

"And a good thing too, by the sounds of it. Yes, very well, if you think these men will have something constructive to add, by all means send for them. Vortrix, thank you for your intelligence this morning. Please go and tell the men that Centurion Corvo has requested their presence and then go and get yourself something to eat and have a rest. When I get a chance, I will see if we can spare you a horse so that you can return to your comrades at Fort Otto."

"Thank you, Legate. However, if the centurion's plan involves going back to the tribesmen's camp, then I would request permission to accompany them instead of returning to Camp Otto. I am after all, the last of my unit left alive. Besides, while I have shown you on the map where their camp is, nobody knows the forest better than me and a detour may become necessary."

The legate looked at Corvo, leaving the decision to him.

"Very well, fetch the men and then join us, Vortrix. I too think you will be of some use, but only if you are up to it physically. You've had a rough time of it of late."

The Gaul straightened as if insulted by the insinuation. "I will not let you or anybody else down, Centurion, of that I can assure you."

"I don't doubt it. Go and fetch the other men, and then together we'll see about getting you some vengeance, perhaps."

Vortrix smiled, the notion of vengeance bringing him some comfort. Then he turned and headed out the door to find Galba, Flavius and Atilus — the man who had saved his life.

Half an hour later, Corvo had finished outlining his plan and stood looking at the other men around the table. Most of their faces were hard to read, but he could see Atilus and Vortrix approved, though Corvo suspected any plan which gave the Gaul an opportunity to kill tribesmen would appeal to him.

"Well, what do you think, men?" asked the legate.

"I think it's just mad enough to work," said Flavius.

"With a little modification, yes, I agree," said Galba.

"Anyone else?" asked the legate.

The rest of the men gathered around the table nodded their approval.

"I have to ask, Centurion: given last night's events, can you count on your men?" asked the legate. He was referring to the bloody altercation involving Traianus and his friends.

"Most of them, yes. Atilus' gladiators save for one or two exceptions are steadfast. My regulars and veterans are all good men. It is only Traianus and his men I do not completely trust, though in fairness they stood their ground in the battles we have fought together so far."

"If there is any doubt, perhaps you should leave them behind?"

"That would be the safest course of action, I agree, but they make up around a third of my force, so in truth I need them. There is also the small matter of how many of them will stay at my side once I hand them their pardons later today."

"You're still going through with that?" asked the legate, surprised.

"Of course. We promised them pardons and freedom upon the successful completion of our mission. Returning Gaius here was just that. I am honour-bound to uphold my end of the bargain."

"But what if the majority take their freedom and go? How will we execute your plan then?"

"I'd make it work somehow, Legate. Besides, I suspect that few if any will leave our ranks with the promise of coin tantalisingly close."

"Until they hear what they've got to do in order to earn it," said Flavius ruefully.

"True, but let's be honest, where are they going to go? We're surrounded by enemies. It is safer to stay with us, hopefully earn their reward and then march out of here with their freedom and heads held high come the spring."

"I hope you are right, Centurion," said the legate.

"Well, we shall see, as I will be calling a parade to impart the good news after the noon meal."

The promise of sun just after dawn had soon given way to cloud, which hung around until noon, but by the time both Corvo's and the garrison's men were standing on parade, they were bathed in the weak sunshine of an early winter afternoon. The officers had debated long and hard over whether to give Corvo's men their manumissions in front of the garrison or to do it discreetly, out of sight. The legate and others had been concerned that allowing the garrison men to witness the presentation of the manumissions might serve only to fuel the tensions between the two camps. Corvo had argued that to do it in secret would just cause suspicion and bad feeling when the garrison men found out, which they surely would in no time at all. In the end, Corvo had won the argument. They had also discussed whether to share the mission plans with the men, but this time they had unanimously decided to just tell them the objective and not the details. All they needed to know was that they were going to attempt to retrieve the pay chest. He suspected that would be enough to hold their attention. Nevertheless, he knew that one day soon, there would be a reckoning between the garrison soldiers and Traianus' men.

Corvo climbed up onto the northern rampart and spared a quick glance across the clearing towards the forest edge, wondering how many pairs of eyes were eagerly watching him from within its gloomy depths. The idea of turning his back on the forest to address the men gathered in the square below did not fill him with joy. However, he had made a big play of encouraging the legate to trust his men, so he could hardly now complain that he in turn didn't trust the legate's men to keep watch. He had no doubt that the sentries would be listening keenly to everything he said; he just hoped they kept their gazes firmly fixed on the treeline while they did.

Corvo cast his gaze across the two sets of men and nodded. "Legion of The Damned," he began and noticed that some of the legate's men smirked or openly mocked the name his men had awarded themselves. He chose to ignore them. "When I first recruited you, I made you two promises. To those that were serving time in a penal colony or prison, I promised a pardon. To those I took from a ludus, I promised freedom, which I also promised the slaves among you. I also promised you all, citizen of Rome, convict or slave, that you would be rewarded with silver." Cheering broke out among Corvo's men, but looks of discontent were evident on the faces of the garrison men. "In that box down there —" he pointed to where a small wooden box rested on the ground between Centurion Galba and Optio Nerva — "are the papers granting your freedom or pardons. From this moment on, I no longer see gladiators, slaves, and prisoners; all I see are free men, men who earned their freedom with acts of bravery, and for that I salute you." A few men cheered, but not as many as Corvo had hoped. Nor had the cheering been that enthusiastic. He began to worry that he had made the wrong choice.

"Where's the box containing the silver, Centurion?"

The shout had come from someone among Corvo's men, but he did not recognise the voice. Traianus was smirking and Corvo instantly knew that it had been one of his men, no doubt put up to it by the man himself.

"Probably in some barbarian's tent, along with our missing pay chest!" called out Batilus. The men around him burst into bitter laughter. The legate glared at Batilus but said nothing. This was Corvo's moment.

"You were promised it, and you shall receive it." More cheering, a little louder this time. "But first you've got to earn it." The cheering instantly stopped as the men started to shout and grumble. Nerva looked at Corvo to see if he wanted him to silence the men and bring them back to order, but Corvo gestured that he was content to let their complaining run its course and die out.

"We've already earned it, Centurion. The proof is standing right over there, next to the legate," called Bora, one of the gladiators Corvo had recruited. He pointed at Tribune Crispus standing next to his father.

"You have, and any man who wants to take his pardon and march out of these gates is free to do so with my blessing, but if he does, he relinquishes his right to receive his share of silver. The baggage train carrying the pay chest for the Twenty-Second was attacked and its escort murdered. The silver which was to be used to reward you was also in that chest. The legate and his men have been trying to locate it ever since. Yesterday, two Gaulish cavalrymen who had been taken prisoner by the local tribesmen managed to escape. One of them is standing over there, but the other one was unfortunately slain outside these very walls last night." Corvo pointed to where Vortrix was standing, looking self-conscious.

"What does any of this have to do with the missing silver?" asked one of Traianus' men, though Corvo noted that the garrison men were nodding their agreement.

"I'm getting to that. Vortrix —" Corvo again pointed to the Gaul — "was being held captive in the tribe's camp. While there, he saw that they had the pay chest." Quiet conversation rippled through the gathered men. "We're going to go and get it back."

"That's impossible!" shouted another man who Corvo didn't see.

"The gate is over there. If you wish to have no part in it, you can collect your manumission and leave now with both my and the legate's gratitude. Step forward any man who wishes to leave. There is no shame or disgrace. You have done everything and more that I asked of you and have earned your freedom." Nobody moved. "Be sure, because I will not make this offer again. If you stay, then you are here for the duration of this new mission." Again nobody moved. "Very well, you have all chosen to stay. The men under my command, go and collect your papers from Centurion Galba unless you wish us to hold onto them for safekeeping. The rest of you, check your kit and get yourselves ready, because soon we are going to get back our silver."

This time the cheering was loud and genuine, and carried all the way to the forest edge.

CHAPTER 6

It was a gamble, Corvo knew that. They all did. If things did not go as they planned, and there was every chance that they wouldn't, every Roman north of the Rhenus would be killed and their heads taken as trophies. It was not a comforting thought. Yet Corvo believed that they had little choice. The nights were drawing in and the temperature was plunging, heralding the onset of another brutal northern winter. If they didn't act soon, the weather would prevent them from being able to do so until the spring thaw, and by then it would be too late. Discontent within the forts was rife, none more so than in Fort Felix, and the prospect of mutiny grew stronger every day.

It had taken several days, but once the senior officers had agreed upon the finer details of the plan, Centurion Jovian was summoned from Fort Duma. The experienced centurion listened intently as Corvo explained the plan to him. He asked pertinent questions where necessary but seemed content.

"So, what do you think, Centurion?" asked Corvo when he had finished outlining the plan for what felt like the hundredth time.

Accustomed to obeying orders rather than being asked for an opinion, Jovian was momentarily taken aback, and the startled expression that swept across his face made Corvo grin.

"If you're asking me for an honest opinion, and I believe you are, there is a whole host of things that could go wrong, any one of which could see the plan unravel, but I don't see we have much choice. We need to do something and soon. The atmosphere within Duma is tense and dangerous. I lost another four men over the walls the other night."

"Deserters?" asked Arus.

"Yes. They're not the first and I suspect they'll not be the last if we don't do something."

"Did your patrols catch them?" asked the legate. Centurion Jovian looked uncomfortable and glanced nervously at Arus. "Well, Centurion?"

"I told him to cease all patrols until further notice," said Arus. "I meant to tell you, but with everything that's been happening it slipped my mind."

The legate's eyes narrowed as he stared at his old friend. "Did you now?"

"I did. If every patrol was meeting the same fate as the one Centurion Jovian was leading when we ran into him, then Fort Duma would soon be short of a garrison. I thought it wiser to stop all patrols until I had a chance to speak with you."

The anger in the legate's eyes faded as quickly as it had appeared. "And you were right to do so. Besides, thanks to Vortrix we now know where the pay chest is, so further patrols are unnecessary."

Corvo watched an expression of relief flit across Jovian's face. Arus' face remained impassive. He might have been the legate's fixer and subordinate to him, but clearly he was no stranger to challenging the legate's orders, Corvo realised. It was something he would have to bear in mind in future. Perhaps Arus answered to someone higher up the chain of command.

"Well then, it seems that if we don't act soon, we won't have enough men to carry out the plan anyway," said the legate ruefully.

"What happens if the pay chest is no longer within the camp?" asked Tribune Ortius. It was the question that had been on the lips of many of those attending the briefing.

"Then we are all dead men, I expect, because if the barbarians don't get us, our own men surely will," replied the legate.

"Let's pray to the gods that it is then, but I suggest nobody entertains the notion that the silver is no longer there. If anybody outside this room asks, you just tell them that our latest intelligence confirmed that it is, but don't elaborate," suggested Arus.

"Quite. Any more questions? No? Then we go the day after tomorrow. That gives you time to safely travel back to Duma, Centurion Jovian, and for you to assume your command at Fort Otto, Tribune Ortius. Remember, men, plenty of noisy drills tomorrow. I want the enemy's eyes fixed firmly on your forts. Let them worry what we're up to for a change. Then at first light the day after tomorrow, you march out, making it look like we're abandoning the forts and leaving, which in a manner of speaking I suppose we are."

"Shouldn't we burn them, Legate?" asked Flavius.

"If I was planning on permanent abandonment, yes, but at some point in the future I intend to move back in."

"But what if the tribesmen occupy them in our absence?"

"I don't think they will. They prefer living in their camps among the trees. But if they did, it would probably mean that our plan has failed and it's no longer our problem. Let those who have betrayed us and sit safely behind stone walls on the other side of the Rhenus worry about that. Besides, there's every chance that the enemy will burn the forts for us once they find they've been duped." Nods of agreement greeted this statement. "May the gods grant us good fortune. Courage and honour."

"Courage and honour," repeated the small group of men as they snapped to attention, saluted the legate and then began to file out of his briefing room.

Only the legate's son, Tribune Crispus, remained behind with his father. Corvo lingered outside and overheard their exchange.

"What is it, Gaius?" asked the legate.

"Why have you not given me command of Fort Duma?" asked Tribune Crispus. "I outrank Centurion Jovian."

"I know you do, but Jovian knows the men there and I worry that you are not yet recovered from your ordeal in Armenia."

"I am not, but I am fit enough to take command of a small fort garrison, especially with Jovian there to guide me."

The legate sighed. "Look, Gaius, in all honesty, I am not sure this plan will work — our chances are remote and rely on the gods favouring us, something they have been reluctant to do of late. If we are to die in this place, I would have you at my side rather than half a day's march to my east. I have only just got you back; I cannot risk losing you all over again. Besides, you will be of great use to me here, and I suspect we will not be without our own troubles. Please, don't fight me on this."

Tribune Crispus' voice grew gentle. "I understand, Father."

"Good, now go and see to your men, Tribune. We have much to do."

The next day saw a hive of activity across the three forts. Both Tribune Ortius and Centurion Jovian had safely returned to their respective commands at Fort Otto and Fort Duma the night before. Now, with one day to go before the plan was to be put into action, both men had set about organising the troops under their command. While half of the garrison noisily drilled and carried out weapons practice, the other half cleaned and prepared their kit. Then, after the noon meal, the two groups swapped roles so that by the time the evening meal came, every man was ready to march out the following morning, his kit prepared and his weapons sharpened. It would not have escaped the notice of any tribesmen watching from the trees that something big was going on within the forts, and the Romans knew this would have been communicated back to the tribesmen's camp. They would now be on edge, wondering what the Romans were up to.

Meanwhile, back at Fort Felix, the legate and his son had set about preparing and bolstering the fort's defences. Buckets containing arrows were placed evenly along the west, east and northern walls, as were javelins. Rocks and anything else which could easily be picked up and hurled down at an attacking force, were also stacked in little piles at strategic places along the ramparts.

For Corvo and his men, it was an all too familiar sight and brought back memories of the successful defence they had put up at Fort Lipa in Armenia. Heavily outnumbered, he and his men, together with the small garrison stationed there, had held the enemy off for far longer than they had expected to. Their supply of arrows and javelins exhausted, the beleaguered troops had been preparing to make a final stand, when a Roman legion came marching over the horizon as part of an invasion force from Syria. The enemy, with victory tantalisingly within their reach, had been forced to withdraw.

While the legate was busy preparing Fort Felix's defences, Corvo and his closest officers, together with Atilus, were finalising details for their part in the next day's mission.

"I think bringing Traianus is a mistake," said Atilus.

"We don't really have a choice," replied Corvo.

"I do not trust either him or his men. Why not leave them behind and just bring garrison men with us?"

"Given the trouble and the unresolved murder the other night, I do not feel comfortable leaving Traianus and all his men behind. The gods only know what trouble they might stir up while we're gone. We could come back and find a slaughter."

"We might also find a gladius slipped into our own backs if we are not careful," said Atilus bitterly. "Having Traianus with us is folly enough, but to also have that hot-head Batilus and some of his men is just madness. They have unresolved bad blood with Traianus and his men."

"I know that none of you are happy about them coming with us, and ideally I would not be taking them, any of them. But this is far from an ideal situation, and at this moment in time I would rather keep Traianus and his men where I can see them. And yes, I agree about Batilus, but the legate said that he and some of the other garrison troops had to come, or they might have mutinied. They don't trust Traianus any more than we do and didn't want him left alone with their silver."

"It is your command, Centurion, but I still think you are making a mistake."

"It is done. We will just have to make the best of it. Titus, I would like you to remain behind and assist the legate with the defence of this place."

Galba looked stunned. "Remain behind? But I thought that was all sorted and I was to be part of your section?"

"I know, but on reflection I think the legate could use a good centurion at his side. His son is young and although he was there at Fort Lipa, he did not really get involved in its defence until the last. You were there throughout. You know what it takes to defend a place like this, and you will be a great help to the legate and tribune. Arus will be there too, but organising the defence of a fort isn't his strong point either. They need you, my friend."

Galba took a deep breath. "Very well, I shall remain here and do as you command. Just don't go getting yourself killed!"

"Believe me, I will be trying my hardest not to. Right, I think we've talked this to death. A drink to success?"

"I thought you were never going to ask," said Flavius as he reached over to retrieve a wine jug he had spied earlier sitting next to some empty cups. Flavius poured everyone a healthy measure and they all picked up a cup.

"To another successful mission for The Damned," said Corvo.

"To The Damned," the men echoed before downing their drinks. Then, one by one they filed out of the room to make their final preparations.

Two hours before dawn, out of sight of any watching eyes in the forest, half a dozen men crept over the southern walls of each of the three forts, before stealthily making their way round to the north side. Cloud had rolled in a couple of hours earlier, all but obscuring the moon and smothering its light. Corvo had taken it as a good omen. After checking everyone was all right, each section leader gave a silent signal, and the men began to quietly make their way across the clearings to the trees opposite.

Although every effort had been made to ensure the gates were well lubricated, Corvo had decided that rather than risk an errant squeak betraying their movements, he would order the men to rope-climb out of the forts. He did not know the men leading the sections out of Duma and Otto, but had specifically requested that Legionary Gemmellus be lent to him from Fort Duma to act as the leader of the Fort Felix scouts.

Corvo had been so impressed with Gemmellus' tracking and infiltration skills that there was no one he would have trusted more to get the job done.

Long before the first rays of sunlight peeped over the eastern horizon, all three scouting parties safely reached the forest without being detected. The party out of Fort Duma located the three tribesmen they were looking for almost immediately, stumbling across them as they slept. Had one of them been awake, as they were surely meant to be, the whole plan could have been ruined. Instead, the Romans quietly melted back into the trees, from where they could watch the enemy lookouts with little chance of being discovered themselves.

The men out of Fort Otto struggled to find the enemy lookouts watching their fort and began to panic. Hope was fading as quickly as the cover of darkness, when a movement some fifty paces to their left caught their attention. The section leader let out a quiet sigh of relief when one of the enemy stood up to go and relieve himself in some nearby bushes. Close by, the Romans took up concealed positions from where they too could watch these three enemy lookouts without fear of detection.

It was the men out of Fort Felix that struggled the most. Gemmellus found two of the lookouts easily enough, but the third had wandered off somewhere and the Romans had to be extra vigilant as they took up positions behind the tribesmen in case the missing man suddenly appeared behind them. Their patience paid off, however, as eventually the third man appeared from the east of their position, though where he had been and what he had been doing was not evident.

All was now in place, and the three squads of Romans settled down to await their moment.

Although they didn't speak the tribesmen's language, it was clear to most of the watching Romans that the lookouts were becoming quite agitated and were starting to argue with one another. The Roman section leaders from Duma and Otto both came to the same conclusion, though they were watching different lookouts about a day's march apart — some of the lookouts clearly wanted to send a message back to their chieftain about the increased activity. The others didn't, it seemed, and again both Roman section leaders independently came to the same conclusion — they had nothing definite to report and probably didn't want to risk inviting their chieftain's wrath. They would wait until they had something conclusive to report.

It was exactly what Corvo had hoped would happen; his plan hinged on that reaction. The first gamble had paid off.

Outside Fort Felix, Gemmellus' party continued to observe the three Germani lookouts. The eldest stared intently at the fort's walls, studying the activities along its ramparts. Apparently satisfied that there was nothing unusual going on, he walked over to where his two comrades were sitting, eating and drinking. He said something to one of them, a man perhaps in his mid-twenties, though it was hard to tell his age beneath his long, lank hair and the full beard that covered his face. He seemed to reply dismissively; whatever he said to the older warrior was not well received and resulted in a brutal kick that knocked the food and drink out of his hands. The younger warrior leapt to his feet, his eyes blazing with anger. Unfazed, the older warrior stepped right up to him, grinning malevolently as if daring the younger man to challenge him. The younger warrior seemingly held his gaze for longer than the other man liked, and was rewarded with a powerful strike across the face. The younger man didn't go down, but the watching Romans could see blood trickling out of the corner of his mouth. Anger briefly flared again, but then he seemed to regain control over himself. He looked around, sullenly picked up his spear and after a last venomous glare at the older warrior, who was glowering back at him, he turned and walked into the trees.

Gemmellus silently signalled for one of his party to follow the young warrior and was relieved when the man made a silent departure. In front of them, the older warrior's glare had turned on the remaining tribesman, a young boy of maybe eighteen summers. He had wisely looked away the moment he felt the other man's gaze settle upon him. The older warrior grunted in satisfaction, happy that his authority had been restored, and then walked back to the forest edge to resume his vigil. Meanwhile, his chastised comrade hurried away, the legionary who had been ordered to follow him not far behind.

The legionary returned shortly. Gemmellus looked his way and raised his eyebrows in question. The legionary made a walking motion with two of his fingers and then pointed off towards the north. Gemmellus understood that the legionary was telling him that the third lookout was heading north and was unlikely to be back anytime soon. It was time to act.

Signalling to the men around him, Gemmellus silently got to his feet. The men had been holding their gladii for some time, as they didn't want the enemy to hear the tell-tale squeak as they drew their weapons. Gemmellus signalled for the men to follow him.

While Gemmellus had been silently communicating with his comrades, the older tribesman had returned to watching the fort. He summoned his younger comrade, seemingly uneasy. Clearly not wishing to antagonise the older man, the young warrior hurried over to where he was standing.

Now was their chance, Gemmellus realised. Both men had their backs to them and would be easy kills. The six men advanced on the two Germani, and just when they thought they would take them by surprise, one of the men with Gemmellus got careless and trod on a twig. Despite the heavy rain they had endured lately, the twig was dry and gave a satisfying crack as his weight broke it in two.

Both of the tribesmen begun to slowly turn. Neither reached for their weapons, but the older one spoke with anger, not that Gemmellus understood what he said. It seemed to Gemmellus that the older warrior thought the man he had been quarrelling with a short while before had returned, possibly to continue the argument. When he found himself confronted by six Romans with weapons drawn, the look of surprise on his face was almost comical. It was only surpassed by the look of shock and pain that replaced it as Gemmellus thrust his sword deep into the man's belly.

Wide-eyed with terror, the younger warrior fumbled with his spear, but before he'd even been able to level it at the Romans, two gladii had pierced his body. Both warriors collapsed silently to the ground.

"The other warrior has left?" Gemmellus asked the legionary who had followed the third man.

"Long gone," confirmed the legionary.

Gemmellus nodded. "Then it is time." He wiped his gladius blade clean on the bearskin of the warrior he had killed and then stepped out from the treeline. Glancing up at the sky, he altered his position slightly until he was sure the sun would reflect off his blade and then began to twist it back and forth. At first, he wasn't sure that anybody watching from the ramparts of Fort Felix had seen him, but then a similar sword glint caught his eye, and he knew his message had been received. Satisfied, he sheathed his gladius and waited.

No more than a hundred heartbeats later, the wooden gates to the fort were pulled open and a stream of men jogged out, snaking across the clearing and making straight for where Gemmellus and his companions were waiting for them. By the time they arrived at the treeline, most of the men were panting hard from the effort required to run while carrying their shields and equipment. The legions were known as Rome's heavy infantry for a reason, but the men were generally in good shape, and nobody faltered or dropped back.

"All went well?" asked Corvo when he saw Gemmellus.

"Exactly as you wanted, Centurion. We waited for one of them to go and make his morning report, which should be that nothing unusual is happening at the fort, and once we were sure that he had left, we killed his friends."

"Excellent. Let us hope that exactly the same thing has happened at the other two forts, except there their runners should be reporting that our men have departed both forts and are heading south towards the Rhenus crossing."

"Won't they take the forts when they find them empty?" asked Gemmellus. Like most of the men in the forts, he was not privy to the full plan.

"Probably, but by then the men from Otto and Duma should have arrived at Felix. They will not take that one so easily."

"So we're not crossing the Rhenus," said Gemmellus. The larger picture was starting to make sense. "Your plan is to draw their warriors away from their camp to pursue what they think are our fleeing men, while you and your section raid their camp and steal back the pay chest."

Corvo nodded. "Well done, Legionary Gemmellus. We'll make an officer of you yet. I just hope the chieftain doesn't see through my plan quite as easily as you have, or we're going to find ourselves in a tricky situation."

"But what if their chieftain sends men to watch this fort?"

"Why would he? His scout will have reported nothing is happening here. At worst he should just send a fresh lookout back to update the men here and to warn them to be extra vigilant. If we run into him on our journey, we will kill him. If we don't, by the time he finds his dead comrades and decides to run to one of the other forts, it will be too late, and we should be on our way back to Felix. All we have to do then is avoid them on the way back."

"You make it sound so easy, Centurion."

"That's because in theory it is." Corvo glanced around and saw that his men seemed to have recovered somewhat. "It's time to move. From this point on, keep noise to an absolute minimum. Vortrix will be leading the way, but remain vigilant. We anticipate the war bands will be heading towards Otto or Duma, or perhaps both, but in case the chieftain is cleverer than I think, keep your eyes open and your mouths shut."

"And if you're wrong and the war bands come for Felix and run straight into us, what then, Centurion?" Predictably, it was Traianus who offered the challenge.

"Then things will get interesting." Corvo bit back a comment about whether Traianus and his men would run. "Now, let's go. Vortrix, remember, don't take us to their camp via the most direct route, in case they are heading this way, because that's the route they would take for sure. Take us there as quickly as you can by a different route, understand?" The big Gaul nodded. "Good, then let's go."

The Gaul turned and headed off into the trees, everyone falling into step behind him.

A half day's march to their west and east, the garrisons at Forts Otto and Duma had left their barracks shortly after dawn under the watchful gaze of the Germani lookouts. When they had watched for long enough to judge that it was the entire garrison leaving, both sets of lookouts despatched a runner back to their camp while the others remained to keep watch. In a replay of what had happened outside Fort Felix, the remaining lookouts were then killed by the watching Romans, and signals were sent to the garrisons. The men sent to kill the Germani lookouts then hurried back across the clearings to rejoin their comrades in the march to Fort Felix.

The ruse was on, and the Romans were committed. There was no turning back now.

CHAPTER 7

Despite the onset of winter, many of the tall beech trees so prevalent in the forests of Germania still retained their leaves. Together with the numerous pine trees, whose sweet scent provided welcome relief from the smell of decay and damp that permeated the forest floor, they provided a dense canopy through which the weak daylight struggled to make its presence felt. The sky was turning grey as swollen clouds rolled in from the east, bringing with them the threat of yet more rain. When Vortrix gave the signal to halt, all of these things made it difficult for Corvo to gauge the hour of the day, but he settled on it being a little after mid-morning. He eased his way past the men in front of him until he reached Vortrix's side. The Gaul was crouching down and didn't turn when Corvo appeared and crouched beside him.

"What is it?" Corvo asked quietly as his eyes scanned the area around them.

"Someone is coming. Heading straight for us."

Corvo turned and urgently signalled for his men to crouch down and remain silent. "How many?"

"One."

"Must be their relief sentry." A few moments later a warrior aged about thirty, with a short beard and long blond hair, came strolling into view, not appearing to be in any hurry. That was good, Corvo told himself — it meant that the tribesmen were not concerned about this part of the forest. This was reinforced by the casual way the warrior walked and carried his spear; it was clear that he did not feel threatened and was not expecting any trouble.

He was wrong, and his complacency would cost him his life.

Corvo whispered instructions to Vortrix and after signalling for his men to remain hidden and silent, he moved quickly and silently to his left. When the warrior was no more than ten paces away from him, still oblivious to the imminent danger he was in, Corvo stepped out from his concealed position, brandishing his gladius. For a moment, the warrior did nothing but stare, the shock of finding a Roman so far from the fort and seemingly alone paralysing him with indecision. When Corvo took a menacing step towards him, however, he lowered his spear and prepared to fight.

After a moment, the warrior seemed to realise that Corvo probably wasn't alone after all. He needed to warn the chieftain. He raised his spear and turned to run back to the camp, but all he found when he turned was the snarling face of Vortrix blocking his way. Before he could react to this new threat, Vortrix had thrust his gladius into the tribesman's stomach, right up to the hilt.

The spear dropped from the warrior's grasp as the auxiliary violently jerked his gladius blade from left to right, slicing the man's innards, a look of cruel satisfaction on his face.

"That was for Erdika," Vortrix spat as he tugged his gladius free.

The tribesman gave one last gurgle as blood oozed out of his mouth and then he dropped to the ground, his innards starting to slip out of the gaping wound. Vortrix stepped to the side, a look of disgust on his face, and wiped his blade clean on the dead man's clothes. Then he grabbed him under the shoulders and dragged his body into the deep foliage to his right. Anybody deliberately searching for him would have no trouble locating his body, but there was a good chance that any war band passing through wouldn't notice it. Vortrix then picked up the dead warrior's spear and after hefting it in his right hand, he appeared pleased and decided to keep it.

"How much farther to their camp?" asked Corvo.

"Not far at all. We will be there by noon."

"Good," said Corvo, nodding. He quickly walked over to where Atilus and Nerva crouched and informed them. They in turn informed their men. While Vortrix went off to scout ahead, everyone took the opportunity to quench their thirst and hastily eat something if they were hungry. When Vortrix returned, Corvo gave the signal to silently move out and once again the column fell into step behind the Gaul.

They had actually been closer to the enemy camp than Corvo realised, and he was suddenly very grateful that the sentry they had run into a short time ago had not thought to cry out. If he had, Corvo suspected the noise may well have carried all the way there and the area would now be swarming with hostile tribesmen.

Corvo, Nerva, Atilus and Flavius huddled together in a patch of dense scrub surrounding the clearing in which the tribesmen had set up camp, while the men remained out of sight further back. The four men watched the activity within the camp for some time, trying to gauge the layout and to judge how many warriors were there. Vortrix had returned from his scouting trip and reported that the war band had indeed left the camp, their tracks easy to find. Judging by the direction they were heading in, it was likely that they were heading towards Fort Otto. The chieftain did not seem to have split his forces. He was either a very cautious leader or he knew that if the Romans truly were withdrawing, they only had one place to go. That thought troubled Corvo. He could deal with a cautious leader, but a well-informed one was a different matter.

"How many, do you think?" Corvo asked nobody in particular.

"Twenty to thirty, I should think," replied Flavius.

"And they all look to be grey beards," said Atilus.

"Might be more in the huts," said Nerva.

"There are no perimeter guards, though," Atilus observed. "They clearly think they are untouchable here."

"Well, we're going to shatter that illusion for them," said Corvo with a smile.

"That must be the chieftain's tent," said Nerva, pointing. "It's the only one with guards outside it."

The others followed Nerva's outstretched arm and saw the hut he was pointing at, where two men, warriors past their prime and perhaps deemed too old to join the war band, stood guard on either side of the entrance.

"The chieftain has stayed behind while his war band marches out?" queried Flavius.

"Not likely. He wouldn't remain a chieftain for very long if he did. Warriors only follow a brave man, not one who skulks in his hut while his men fight his battles. No, I would guess that it is not the chieftain they guard but the silver," said Atilus thoughtfully.

"I think you may be right," said Corvo, scratching the stubble on his chin. "All right, remember the plan. In and out as quickly as we can. Kill all the guards and secure the perimeter. Kill only those we need to. It looks like the camp is mostly populated by women, children and old men. If they resist, kill them, otherwise try and take them prisoner. There are two horses tied up over there; we'll use them to carry what silver we can. If we can't bring it all, so be it. We can't tarry here a moment longer than necessary in case this chieftain is wiser than I give him credit for and decides to double back.

Any questions?" The others all shook their heads. "Then good luck, and may the gods smile favourably on us."

Corvo remained where he was while the other three quietly returned to their sections for a final briefing. A few moments later, Corvo sensed the men in his section sidling up behind him. He turned and saw Batilus and some of the garrison men along with Felix and Fabianus, both of whom had been with Traianus at the quarry. Vortrix had also decided to latch onto Corvo's section.

"You ready?" he asked them. They all nodded. To his right, Corvo could see Flavius looking in his direction, awaiting the order to attack. Corvo glanced one last time at the peaceful camp in front of them and opened his mouth to give the order, but before he could do so, a woman's scream pierced the air. Corvo looked in her direction just in time to see a pilum slam into her chest. She was dead long before her body hit the ground.

The air was instantly filled with the sound of screams and shouting as panicked women dashed about the camp, scooping up young children before running to safety. The old men left to guard the camp reached for their weapons but were slow to organise. In accordance with the plan, the Romans poured into the camp from four separate places. Corvo and his section made straight for the chieftain's hut, while Flavius' and Atilus' sections dealt with any warriors who decided to put up a fight. Nerva's section, which consisted predominantly of Traianus and his men, was tasked with securing the perimeter of the camp.

Corvo and his section were no more than seventy paces from the chieftain's hut and things were going well, when suddenly an enormous warrior emerged from the hut to their left. He was perhaps in his late forties but built like an ox and evidently not wanting for courage. Corvo barely had time to register the man's presence before his two-handed war axe was swinging through the air towards his head. The legionary behind Corvo had seen what was about to happen and had shoved Corvo out of the way just in time, but he had misjudged the arc of the swing, and the axe blade tore through his upper arm, severing it just below the shoulder. The legionary screamed with pain and collapsed to the ground, blood spurting out of the wound at an alarming rate.

Another of the garrison men with Corvo had turned to engage the warrior, but the warrior's reactions had been too quick for him, and he had punched the iron head of his axe into the legionary's chest, sending him crashing to the ground winded. Instantly the Germani warrior raised his axe, ready to bring it slamming down into the man's torso, but he in turn suddenly rocked backwards as a spear punched through his tunic and chainmail and sent him stumbling backwards. Incredibly, the warrior did not fall and with a roar of defiance, he mustered the strength to raise his axe once again. Quick as a flash, Corvo leapt behind him and plunged his gladius into the man's back before leaping out of the way. As he had anticipated, the warrior had instinctively swung round, his axe cutting horizontally through the air at head height exactly where Corvo had been standing just moments before. Three more gladii were thrust into the warrior's back, and as he vainly tried to lift his axe one more time, his gaze fell on Corvo. The centurion watched as the light slowly left the man's eyes and he collapsed face-first into the dirt. Even though he knew that the warrior had to be dead now, Corvo was nevertheless wary as he stepped forward and pulled his gladius from the man's back.

All around him, the sounds of battle rang out. Men shouted, women screamed, and children cried. The noise was overwhelming, and Corvo prayed to any gods that might be listening that the chieftain's war band were too far away to hear or react.

The two guards standing outside the chieftain's hut hefted their weapons in readiness. They had watched their comrade die at the hands of the Romans and clearly knew that their turn would come soon.

A young girl of perhaps seventeen or eighteen summers, her dress torn and her breasts exposed, ran screaming past the chieftain's guards, chased by two laughing Romans. With nothing but lust on their minds, both were oblivious to the men watching on either side of them, whether comrade or foe. Out of sight, but not far from where Corvo stood, the Romans had evidently caught their prey, as another scream, different in pitch, rent the air. This was followed by a man's howl of pain and another scream. Then it went silent.

Corvo was seething. He had specifically given orders that there was to be no rape carried out. He knew that it was common for the victorious army to sate its lust on a conquered people and he had witnessed it many times before, though he'd never partaken himself. Normally he would have turned a blind eye, but they were here to do a specific job and didn't have time to waste. If he could identify the culprits when they returned to Fort Felix, he would make them very sorry for disobeying his orders, regardless of whose men they were.

The two warriors standing outside the chieftain's hut had watched the chase and one had even made to go and help the girl, but his comrade had grabbed his arm and restrained him. She was beyond help and was no doubt one of many suffering the same fate. The girl's terror seemed to firm his resolve, and he whispered something to his comrade, who nodded and then turned to glare at Corvo and his men. Adjusting their weapons, both men took a step forward and braced for battle, signalling their intent. There was to be no running away for them, only death and glory.

Corvo began to advance on the two guards and as he did so, he sensed rather than saw his men fan out on either side of him in a line. They had closed in to within thirty paces when a man to Corvo's right went down, an arrow protruding from his chest. By the time the Romans had spotted the archer, they were already nocking another arrow. Two of Batilus' men charged, but the archer was quick. An arrow took the man on the left in the throat, and he dropped to the ground dead. The archer turned to flee, but the remaining legionary was already upon him and thrust his gladius deep into his exposed back. The archer, no more than a youth, dropped to the ground dead.

The legionary had turned and started to make his way back to the formation when a woman let out a high-pitched shriek and came running out from behind one of the huts. She landed on the legionary's back, her legs wrapped around his waist and her left arm around his neck. Before he could dislodge her, she had already plunged a knife she'd been holding into the exposed flesh above his armour several times. As the legionary collapsed with the woman on top of him, Batilus rushed over and despatched the woman with a deep slice across her throat. She collapsed onto the already dead legionary.

Batilus warily made his way back over to Corvo's side. "Even their women are brutal."

"And just as dangerous. Stay alert!" shouted Corvo as he eyed the two guards outside the chieftain's tent, but they managed to advance without further incident.

The two Germani warriors had grinned as they'd watched their kinsfolk kill another three Romans. Hefting their weapons in readiness, they stood a pace apart and braced for an attack.

When the Romans were no more than twenty paces away, one of the two guards said something Corvo didn't understand and a few moments later, two more warriors emerged from the hut. The one who had spoken now grinned as he watched the expressions on the Romans' faces. These two men, although past their prime, were still large and powerful. Numerically, Corvo and his men still held the advantage, but these tribesmen were seasoned warriors and would be worthy adversaries.

"Good. More bastards to kill," said Batilus, making Corvo smile.

Taking a deep breath, Corvo roared and raced forwards, but before they closed in on the tribesmen, the two warriors who had been standing guard outside the hut threw their spears. One took a legionary clean through the centre of his chest, killing him instantly, but the second one was harmlessly deflected as its intended target hastily brought up his shield.

Corvo and the others clattered into the four tribesmen moments later. One of the men who had thrown his spear was too slow to draw his sword and was cut down by a powerful thrust from Fabianus, but the other one had been quicker and had just managed to raise his sword in time to deflect Batilus' powerful thrust.

Corvo, meanwhile, had engaged one of the men who had been hidden in the hut. He had been armed with a spear and was now forcing both Corvo and another of Batilus' men backwards, thrusting with the spear point and keeping them from being able to close in on him and use their short swords.

Corvo knew that if he could just get inside the spear point, the man was his.

Another legionary, this one armed with a pilum, joined them and now three men faced off against the big Germani. The man's face showed no signs of fear, despite now being outnumbered three to one. Instead he just widened his stance so that he could keep all three men at bay.

A shout of pain came from their right and momentarily distracted, the man standing next to Corvo made the mistake of glancing in its direction. It was the opening the Germani had been waiting for, and he immediately seized his chance and thrust forward with his spear. The point punched into the soft spot at the bottom of the legionary's throat. The legionary with the pilum also saw an opportunity and thrust his weapon's point towards the Germani's groin, but the warrior quickly turned even as he was withdrawing his own spear. Instead of piercing the man's groin, the pilum sliced across his thigh, leaving a red gash in its wake. The warrior roared with anger more than pain and swung his spear towards the Roman's legs. Desperate to avoid its point, the Roman tried to take evasive action, but instead just managed to get himself tangled up in the spear shaft and went crashing to the ground. Before the man had time to recover, the tribesman was upon him and rammed the spear deep into his chest.

Corvo saw his moment had finally arrived. With the spear now vertical, he was able to take the opportunity to close in on his adversary. He went in low and sliced the big Germani across the back of his unprotected thigh, hamstringing him and sending him to his knees. But by now the warrior had tugged his spear free, and even as he fell he managed to sweep Corvo's legs from under him, sending him to the ground too. Corvo reacted quickest and before the Germani could bring his spear to bear, he thrust his gladius down through the man's shoulder, right up to the hilt. For one worrying moment Corvo thought the man still lived and in a panic, he stumbled backwards, falling to the ground again. Moments later, without uttering a sound, the Germani warrior collapsed face-first onto the dead legionary in front of him.

Batilus offered Corvo a hand and then hauled him to his feet. Corvo nodded his thanks. Glancing around, he saw that for the moment at least, there were no tribesmen around, Batilus and the others having despatched the remaining two warriors. His gaze fell on the Germani woman lying dead a few strides away, and he reminded himself that the women were potentially as dangerous as the men. Maybe more so. Danger lurked in and behind every hut.

"You men, stand guard out here. Shout if anyone approaches. Batilus, you come with me. Let's go and see how much of the emperor's silver remains, shall we?" Corvo turned and prepared to enter the gloomy hut which they had assumed was used by the chieftain. It was slightly larger than all the others, and half a dozen heads had been thrust onto stakes on either side of the hut's entrance. Corvo looked at them with disgust, then signalled for Batilus to follow him inside as he entered the hut, ducking to avoid hitting his head as he did so.

It was just the entrance that was low; once the two men had entered the hut, they were able to stand upright. They waited for their eyes to grow accustomed to the gloomy interior and then looked about them. Ferns lined the floor, and in the corner a number of furs had been laid on top of each other to make what Corvo assumed was a bed for the chieftain and his wife. Small log cuttings served as seats. Various weapons lay discarded on the ground, some tribal, some Roman, taken from the dead or perhaps from the men whose heads now adorned the hut entrance. Then, at the very back of the hut, Corvo spied the wooden chest that had contained the legion's pay. Batilus had seen it too and the two men hurried over to where it stood, totally at odds with the rest of the hut's contents. No attempt had been made to hide it, suggesting that the chieftain had been confident that none of his men, whether out of respect or fear, would try and steal from it.

The lock had been broken, so Corvo flipped open the lid to reveal a chest full of silver coins. The chieftain had clearly put some other things he treasured in there, as not all of it was silver. Behind Corvo, Batilus issued a long, low whistle.

"Is it all there, do you think?"

"Looks that way. It seems the chieftain has even put some of his own personal wealth in there for safekeeping," replied Corvo.

"Well, I'm sure the men will take good care of it for him," said Batilus with a grin.

"This is going to be heavy to carry unless we can find something to put it in. Horses are no good if we've no saddlebags." Silently Corvo was cursing himself for not having anticipated this problem.

"Legionary Felix, get yourself in here with one of the other men!" barked Batilus.

Moments later, Felix and Fabianus entered the hut. They both stared wide-eyed at the chest brimming with silver. Corvo quickly shut the lid but had no means of securing it. There was no sense in putting temptation in anybody's way.

"What's going on out there?" asked Corvo.

"I think it's over, Centurion," said Felix. "The sounds of battle have died away."

"That is good. The camp must be ours. Think you two can carry that?" Corvo pointed at the chest.

"All the way back to Fort Felix? Not likely," said Fabianus.

"Just outside to the horses. Once we find something to put it in, they can carry it back to Fort Felix."

"They ran," said Felix.

"Who did?" asked Corvo, fearing he meant Traianus and his men.

"The horses. They ran into the trees some time ago."

"Damn it to Hades! All right, you two are going to have to carry it for now. We'll get other men to take a turn if necessary."

"Don't worry, Centurion. I'll carry it myself if I have to," said Felix. He sheathed his gladius and bent to lift the chest. Felix was a mountain of a man, tall for a Roman, with muscles honed from long hours working in the penal quarry. Although, like Fabianus, he was one of Traianus' comrades, he had never shown anything but respect to Corvo and his fellow officers. Nor for that matter had Fabianus.

Felix managed to lift the chest, but it was clear from the look on his face and the way his arms shook that the strain was too much, and he was soon forced to put it back down. Corvo suspected that even with Fabianus' help, he would not be able to carry it very far and certainly not back to Fort Felix. Nor could they afford to keep stopping and swapping porters, as they were going to be vulnerable enough as it was on their return journey and unnecessary delays would not improve their chances.

"Sorry, Centurion," said Felix, looking embarrassed.

"It's all right. Just get it outside between you and we'll work something out. There must be something in this camp we can use to transport it. We'll just have to improvise — maybe separate it into smaller amounts."

"Centurion, you'd better get out here quickly." The call had come from just outside the hut, though Corvo didn't recognise the voice and imagined it was one of Batilus' men. Had the tribesmen returned?

Corvo looked to Batilus, but the older legionary just shrugged. "Follow us out," ordered Corvo, turning to Felix and Fabianus. Corvo then ducked as he stepped outside into the clearing, momentarily shielding his eyes against the light. The men he'd left outside guarding the hut stood where he'd left them, weapons drawn and staring outwards in a defensive posture. But it was not hostile Germani tribesmen facing them, but Corvo's men. Nerva, Atilus and Flavius were all on their knees, as were a number of other men, mostly former gladiators and regular legionaries, although Corvo recognised a couple of former slaves and convicts among them as well. Someone was missing, but he couldn't immediately remember who. None of them were carrying weapons, and behind them stood Traianus and a dozen other men, mostly his comrades from the quarry, but also a couple of thieves they had liberated from prisons. Some, like Traianus, had their gladius point held against a prisoner's throat. Traianus was grinning like a wolf that had trapped its prey.

So finally he makes his move, thought Corvo, weighing up the situation before him. Behind him he heard Felix and Fabianus come puffing and wheezing out of the hut, carrying the chest.

"What in Hades do you think you're doing, Traianus?"

"What does it look like, Centurion?"

"It looks like you're committing suicide, that's what. Let them go — now!"

"I don't take orders from you, Centurion — never really did. None of us did."

"Why do this? Why now? You have your pardons. You were free to lead your own lives again as free men — and now we've found the silver, as wealthy ones too. You're throwing it all away. It doesn't make sense."

Traianus' gaze was fixed on the chest that a struggling Fabianus had been forced to put down.

"So you were right — the silver was here. Well done, Centurion. Trouble is, I'm not very good at sharing. Why should I put up with just some of the silver when I can have it all? Me and the men here will take it now and be on our way."

"Don't be a fool, Traianus — how far do you think you'll get? The chances of all of us getting back were slim, so what chance has a dozen of you got? Where will you even go? To the north there are tribesmen, to the south, west and east, Romans. Your lifespan can probably be measured in hours. Death on a cross or death by painful Germani torture. Your prospects don't look good." Corvo could see that one or two of Traianus' men were faltering. Greed had apparently made them act rashly, and now they were perhaps beginning to regret it. "Throw down your weapons and let the others go, and I will ask the legate to be lenient with you."

Some of them were definitely wavering, and Traianus knew it too. "We'll be fine, Centurion. Don't you worry about us. But you're right — the longer we linger here, the greater the chances of those hairy-backed bastards returning. Felix, Fabianus, bring the chest over here."

"We can take them, Centurion. Just give the order," said Batilus, adjusting his hold on his gladius. On either side of him, Corvo heard the other men in his section do the same.

"Think you're good enough, do you, Batilus?" spat Traianus.

"Oh, I know we are, and I'm coming for you, have no doubts. Either here or somewhere else, I will have my vengeance both for Artorius and the men you betrayed."

"What, like you did in the mess hall the other day? You and your men couldn't fight your way out of a room full of eunuchs." Some of the men behind Traianus laughed, but not all.

"Centurion?" Batilus' temper was rising and Corvo wondered how long it would be before Traianus' provocations made him lose control and kill him. Corvo would have no issue with that; the fact that Traianus and his men might firstly kill some of their captives was a different matter. He continued to weigh their chances in his mind before finally saying, "No, not while they've got our men at sword point."

"And just so you both know, it was me who killed your friend Artorius the other day. He squealed like a pig." Traianus was in full flow now.

"You're a dead man, Traianus!" shouted Batilus, but before he could surge towards the other man, Corvo grabbed him by the shoulder and stopped him. Batilus whirled round to face the centurion, his eyes burning with fury. "What are you doing? You've just heard him admit to murdering my comrade — he's got to pay for it."

"And he will, but not here, not now. Think of the others."

Traianus sneered. "That's right, I could kill any one of these or maybe all of them, so you'd better listen to the centurion if you don't want that to happen. Now, Felix, Fabianus, hurry up and bring that chest over here." Felix glanced at Corvo, who nodded. "Don't look at him!" shouted Traianus, enraged. "I give the orders, not him. You and Fabianus are my men — always have been, remember?"

Felix and Fabianus crouched, picked up the chest and carried it over to where Traianus stood, before setting it down on the ground again.

"We're going to be rich, boys!" shouted Traianus as he used his foot to flip open the lid of the chest. His men cheered, their earlier doubts seemingly having vanished once they caught sight of the silver and treasure crammed inside. "Think of all the whores you'll be able to buy — a different one every night even for you, Albinius."

Albinius, a man of indeterminable age, with half his left ear missing and a nasty scar that travelled from his forehead over his eye and cheek to his chin, smiled, revealing a mouth almost devoid of teeth. The few that remained were black and rotten.

Having set the chest down, Felix and Fabianus made their way back over to where Corvo and his men were standing.

"Felix, Fabianus, what are you doing? Come and join your comrades," said Traianus, incredulous.

Fabianus looked to his big comrade and watched as Felix shook his head slowly and said, "The centurion and the others have kept their promise and granted us our freedom. They have been fair and honourable. What you do here, that is not honourable, and I want no part in it."

"Honour be damned! You can't buy wine and whores with honour. Don't you want the silver? Are you really as stupid as you look?"

"There are more important things than silver. Honour is one such thing."

"Then you are a fool. Stay here and die with these idiots. More silver for us. Now, throw down your weapons, Centurion, all of you, and I'll let these men live."

"Rome will hunt you, Traianus. It never forgets — you know this," said Corvo.

"We shall see. Now, last chance — throw down your weapons or I'm going to start cutting throats."

"Don't do it, Centurion," urged Nerva. "Think of the men back in Felix. If we don't get that silver back, we'll have more trouble on our hands than this bunch of bastards."

"Shut your mouth, Nerva," spat Traianus. "Time's up, Centurion. What's it going to be?"

"Centurion, don't..." Nerva's words were cut short as the man restraining him ran his gladius blade across the optio's throat.

CHAPTER 8

For a few moments everybody, including Traianus, just stared at the sight of Nerva's lifeless body slumped on the ground and bleeding out, his killer standing over him with a bloody gladius in his hand.

The look on Traianus' face betrayed the fact that he thought his comrade had made a mistake. When a javelin slammed into the man's chest, sending him stumbling backwards, he knew it for sure.

The distraction provided Atilus with the opportunity he had been waiting for. Feeling the pressure of the blade against his throat slacken slightly, he used his lightning-fast reflexes and grabbed the wrist of the man standing behind him. Viciously twisting it at the same time, Atilus forced the man's arm up and away from his throat. The gladius dropped to the ground. Atilus was on his feet in moments and still holding the man's arm, he swept the other man's legs out from under him before grabbing the gladius and driving it deep into his chest.

Other men who had been forced to their knees also took the opportunity to break free. Some succeeded, but others were either too slow or not as skilled as Atilus and ended up with a cut throat.

Some of Traianus' men had simply panicked when the javelin had struck their comrade in the chest and had pushed their captive away. Others remained standing, unsure what to do, but when Corvo and his men charged towards them, their nerves broke and they tried to run. Corvo's men were soon upon them, and a bloody battle ensued.

One of Traianus' men took a wild swing at Corvo, but the centurion ducked just in time, the blade clipping his helmet and knocking it from his head. Corvo came in low, his blade biting deep into the man's lower abdomen. It was a killing blow, but the man would not die quickly. Corvo tugged his blade free and moved on to the next man. He made two thrusts towards Corvo, both of which were easily deflected before the man took a pace back. They circled each other warily, each waiting for an opening. Corvo could see in the other man's eyes that he did not relish the fight and was looking for a way out, a way to save his skin.

"It's too late for that," said Corvo. "You picked the wrong side. Now you're going to pay the price."

Clearly disturbed by how the centurion had known what he was thinking, the man's concentration wavered, and he unconsciously lowered his blade. Corvo was on him in a flash, and after pushing the other man's blade out of the way with his gladius, he stamped his right foot into his adversary's knee, pushing it towards his other leg. There was a satisfying crack, and the man collapsed to the ground, screaming in agony. Corvo silenced his cries with a powerful thrust of his gladius into the man's chest.

Around him the sounds of battle seemed to be dissipating, and Corvo took the opportunity to glance about. Perhaps a dozen men lay dead, while others sat or lay on the ground, trying to stem the flow of blood from their wounds. One man had a nasty gash across his forearm, but Corvo thought he would live so long as the wound didn't get infected. Another had been stabbed in the thigh, but again it was not a fatal injury. Another lay with a horrific stomach wound and would soon be dead. His passing would be neither quick nor peaceful.

Clearly realising the futility of their situation, two of Traianus' men threw down their weapons and surrendered, but Batilus and Fabianus simply ran them through with their own weapons. The men collapsed to the ground, expressions of shock etched on their faces. No quarter was being given, and Corvo didn't blame them. Batilus was getting revenge for the death of his friend Artorius, but his lust for vengeance would not be sated until Traianus lay dead at his feet.

"It is over," said Atilus, coming over to where Corvo stood scanning the scene around him.

"How did this happen?"

"Apologies, Centurion. They came at us from behind. They were ordered to secure the perimeter, if you recall, so it was a simple matter for them to close in on us from the rear. We were too busy dealing with the tribesmen in front of us to worry about what was behind us. In hindsight, perhaps Traianus and his comrades were not the best men to cover our backs." There was no accusation in Atilus' words, merely a statement of fact.

"It is not your fault, Atilus. The blame is mine. You tried to warn me, but my ego overruled my common sense. I thought that perhaps he and his men had changed after what we had all been through in Armenia. I was wrong and I apologise. I will not make that mistake again." Corvo glanced about him. "Where is Traianus' body?"

Atilus scanned the ground but could not see him. "By the gods, he must have escaped. He is as slippery as an eel."

"Damn it to Hades! No matter. He has nowhere to go. The tribesmen will no doubt do our work for us when they run into him, as they surely will."

"Three!" said Flavius as he came striding over. He was covered in blood and Corvo's eyes widened in concern for his old friend.

"Lucius! Are you injured?"

"What? No, not my blood."

Corvo breathed a sigh of relief. "Three what?"

"Three of them got away, Traianus and two others. I saw it but couldn't do anything about it, as I was busy," said Flavius, indicating the blood covering his body.

"What of the village inhabitants?" asked Corvo. Atilus raised his eyebrows and Flavius licked his lips, unable to meet his friend's gaze. "Well?"

"I can answer that," said Vortrix, walking over to join the small group.

"Yes?"

"Traianus and his men killed just about all of them."

"What? The women and children?" It wasn't unheard of for Roman soldiers to put whole villages to the sword — Corvo knew this. He had witnessed such barbarity on several occasions across the Empire, and it was usually done as an act of vengeance or to set an example. He had always considered it an unnecessary act of cruelty and it had sickened him. He had given specific orders that only those who offered resistance were to be killed, and once more Traianus had disobeyed his orders. Corvo was furious. If Batilus wanted revenge, he was going to have to wait his turn.

"We managed to save a few … a handful out of a whole village," Vortrix went on. "That is why I wasn't around to be taken captive by Traianus — I was trying to get some of the women and children to safety."

"Lucky for us. That was some throw, my friend," said Atilus, referring to the spear that had killed the man who had cut Nerva's throat.

"All Gauls are proficient with the spear," said Vortrix, shrugging off the praise. "But my skill is not comparable to yours, I think, not after the throw that saved my life."

Atilus grinned and did not contradict the Gaul.

"You also took a risk. Some of their women are as ferocious as the men," said Corvo, remembering the woman who had leapt on the legionary's back and stabbed him repeatedly.

"Not these."

"And where are they now, these villagers?" asked Corvo.

"In one of the huts, being guarded. That is not the worst of it, though, Centurion."

Corvo's eyes widened as he wondered what could possibly be worse. "Explain."

"When I entered one hut, I found Traianus and two of his men. Traianus was raping the chieftain's wife while his men restrained two young boys — her sons. When I tried to intervene, I got this." Vortrix pointed to where his eye was starting to swell. "During the struggle, the eldest of the two boys managed to wriggle free and leapt on Traianus' back. Traianus killed him. The tribe will not come to terms now. It is a fight to the death."

Corvo nodded as he tried to digest this news and was about to ask a question when a shout of warning went up from one of Corvo's men. They all turned just in time to catch a glimpse of someone racing through the camp towards the trees.

"That is the chieftain's youngest son. He is probably going to try and reach the war band," said Vortrix.

Corvo noticed one of his men raise a pilum ready to throw at the boy. "No! Let him go." The legionary lowered his javelin.

"Well, we'd better not still be here if he succeeds in finding them."

"Maybe the child will run into Traianus," offered Atilus.

A couple of heartbeats later, two legionaries and Drax, a former gladiator from the pits of Rome and the first man Corvo had recruited to his force after Flavius, went hurtling into the trees after the boy.

"Come back, you fools! You'll never catch him!" shouted Corvo but his words went unheard or unheeded.

"Let us hope they catch the boy," said Flavius.

"Better that they don't."

Flavius looked at his friend as if he had lost his mind. "If the boy finds his father and brings the war band running back here, we'll…"

"Be long gone and know that they are not in front of us. Think about it. Vortrix said that the war band's tracks were heading towards Fort Otto. If the boy reaches them, they are going to return via the same direct route. That means that we can head back to Fort Felix using our most direct route, safe in the knowledge that we're not going to run into the war band that way."

"Unless the chieftain sees through your plan."

"I am counting on his grief clouding his judgement. An angry man doesn't usually make good decisions."

Flavius nodded. "So what now?" He watched as the back of the last man disappeared into the trees after the chieftain's son.

"Now we find something, anything, to carry this silver in and we make best speed back to Fort Felix," replied Corvo.

"And the dead?"

Corvo shook his head. He didn't give a damn about Traianus and his traitors, they could be food for the carrion, but it pained him to leave good men like Nerva behind. Nerva, the former drill master at the training barracks outside Rome had made Corvo's and countless other legionaries' lives miserable during their time with him. Many had thought Corvo mad when he had recruited him, but Corvo had known that Nerva would be perfect to help him mould the disparate group of regulars, convicts, slaves and gladiators into a fighting force Corvo could be proud of, Traianus notwithstanding. And he had done exactly that. The man deserved better than to be left lying in the forest dirt for that reason alone, never mind the bravery he had displayed in the battles in Armenia. Yet that was what he was going to have to do. They had enough problems working out how to transport the silver; they couldn't add to them by burdening themselves with bodies. The dead were dead and didn't care. He was certain Nerva would have agreed. "We'll have to leave them here."

Flavius looked aghast. "But, Marcus, it's Sextus and a couple of other men who went through it all with us in Armenia. We can't just leave them here."

"Do you think it doesn't pain me, Lucius? I have no choice. I have to look to the living now."

Flavius glanced at Atilus for support, but the former gladiator just stared back, not giving any indication of his thoughts.

"And what about Drax and the others?" asked Atilus.

"If they're back by the time we're ready, then they'll come with us. If they're not, then they're on their own and will have to make their own way back to Fort Felix."

"I for one will not mourn Drax's absence if that comes to pass," said Atilus, smiling.

"Maybe not, but with our losses here and Traianus' betrayal, our numbers are greatly reduced, and whether you liked him or not, Drax could fight."

"He was a killer, I'll grant you that, but he was no fighter."

"Well, we can discuss the finer points of swordsmanship another time, Atilus. Right now, I want to get this silver packed so we can be on our way back to Fort Felix before anything else goes wrong."

A short while later, Corvo was informed that they were ready to move out. Wicker baskets, saddlebags, and anything else that could be used to hold a few coins were liberated from the camp and filled. As Felix had warned him, the two horses had indeed fled, either having been spooked into escaping their tethers, or because somebody had taken pity on them and set them free. Either way, unless they ran into them on the journey back to Fort Felix, they were going to be of no use to Corvo. With considerably less men than he had anticipated having at his disposal, Corvo realised that every man was going to have to carry some silver, officers included. Vortrix would be the exception, as he would be sent ahead to scout the way for them and needed to move quietly and nimbly, neither of which would be possible if he was weighed down by silver coins.

It would be hard work for Corvo and the others and would mean that if they were caught unawares, the men would be slower to react and arm themselves. Yet Corvo saw that he had little choice in the matter. He also suspected that not all of the coins would remain in the bags and that some would end up secreted about some of the men. He didn't blame them. Besides, once a thief, always a thief, though he knew that even his regular soldiers would not be averse to lining their own pockets. The chances for plunder on their mission had been few and far between, and a Roman soldier was only loyal so long as he was being paid. To date, his men had neither been paid nor had the opportunity to plunder. Therefore, he would not deny them a few coins.

There were more surviving villagers than they had originally feared. Many women and young children had been found cowering in huts and beneath rugs. Once a final sweep of the camp had been carried out and Corvo was satisfied that there was unlikely to be anybody else hidden, he ordered the prisoners to be placed in the chieftain's hut. Clearly fearing that the hut was about to be set alight and that they would all be burned alive, the women started to wail, which in turn made the children cry. Corvo winced at the noise and the distance it would carry. He shook his head against the notion that it would perhaps have been safer and wiser to put them all to the sword. Safer, certainly, but not wiser, he decided. He was not sure that he could have lived out his days with that on his conscience. When the villagers realised that they were merely going to be barricaded into the hut but not burned, the wailing and crying subsided, replaced by a pitiful whimpering.

The barricade wouldn't hold them for long, but it didn't need to. Corvo and his men just needed to slip into the forest, away from prying eyes. With nobody among Corvo's men capable of speaking their language, Atilus had tried to impress on the belligerent and sullen-looking prisoners that if they tried to escape the hut before time, they would be shot with an arrow. He had pointed to a Syrian archer by the name of Kochar to reinforce his point, but he had no idea whether the message had got across.

"We're ready to go, Marcus," said Flavius, who found his friend crouched beside the body of Sextus Nerva. Corvo had folded the dead man's arms across his chest and placed his gladius under them. Although he couldn't bear to think about it, Corvo knew that there was every chance that the tribesmen, especially when they saw what Traianus and his men had done to the villagers, would violate the dead Romans' bodies, but there was nothing he could do.

"Have Drax and the others returned?" asked Corvo, standing and rubbing his hands together. Flavius shook his head sadly. "Then we can wait no longer. We'd better…" Before he could finish his sentence, Corvo saw a man come stumbling out of the forest towards them. It was clear from the way he staggered and the blood running down his thigh that he had been in a fight and was wounded. Corvo glanced nervously at the trees behind the man, half expecting a horde of angry tribesmen to come roaring out of the gloom, intent on taking their heads. "Form line."

Instantly the men dropped what they were carrying and raced to form a line of shields and swords behind Corvo.

The wounded man staggered over to where Corvo, Flavius and now Atilus stood and then collapsed to his knees in front of them.

"Drusius," said Flavius, recognising a former slave who had taken to being a legionary with no trouble at all and who held the promise of becoming a fine soldier. "What happened?" Flavius crouched down and held the man upright. He was losing a lot of blood, but it wasn't obvious where the major wound was located among all the other cuts and scrapes.

"We went after that runner … the lad from the hut… He was fast … too fast … and we soon lost him… Coridan said we should head back, and I agreed…" The man's words were coming in short bursts, interspersed with small coughs which led to dark blood seeping from the corners of his mouth. His time was short. "We turned… I heard a grunt … looked to my right and saw…" Another racking cough escaped him, spraying blood on Corvo's legs.

"What did you see, Drusius?" prompted Flavius.

"That bastard gladiator … Drax … he'd run him through with his gladius."

"Drax killed Coridan? Are you sure, Drusius?" asked Corvo, going down on his haunches so he could look into the other man's eyes. The light in them was fast fading. In a matter of moments, he would be on his way to Elysium.

"Turned on me… I tried to hold him off … didn't expect it… He…"

And then he passed. Flavius gently eased the man's body to the ground.

"Why? Why would Drax do that?" asked Flavius pleadingly.

"Because he is a snake from the pits who should never have been allowed to come with us," said Atilus. His eyes met Corvo's, the accusation unspoken. Deep down, Corvo knew Atilus was right.

"But still, there must have been a reason," said Flavius.

"Perhaps he seeks to join Traianus; they are of the same breed of snake," suggested Atilus.

"Then why not join him earlier, when Traianus made his move in the village? No, it's something else." Corvo went quiet for a few moments as he considered the possibilities. "He is Germani. Maybe he's from one of the tribes around here and has some fool notion of being taken back in by them."

"He said he was Chatti. They're not from around here," said Atilus.

"No, farther north, but perhaps he wasn't telling the truth about that either. Perhaps he is in fact from one of the local tribes."

"Well, if he is, they're unlikely to take him back, surely? The scent of Rome is on him."

"Maybe, maybe not. It depends on what he has to offer them. Either way, there is nothing we can do about it now. It's just one more reason to be on our way." Corvo turned to face his diminished and grim-faced men standing in a line behind him. "Pick up your burden, men, but be very vigilant as we make our way back to Fort Felix. It seems we have more enemies than we thought. Move out." Corvo picked up his basket and set off towards Fort Felix, gesturing for Vortrix to lead the way.

CHAPTER 9

Progress was slow. Although Corvo had tried to demonstrate confidence about their journey home, he was mindful of the fact that the chieftain might be able to rein in his emotions and think rationally. If he took but a moment away from his grief and analysed the situation, he would realise that the Romans would be either heading to Fort Felix or one of the river crossings. All he would have to do then was hurry his war band from Fort Otto to cut off the Roman retreat.

Corvo hoped the man's grief was deep.

A few paces ahead of him, Vortrix once again gave the silent signal to halt and for what felt like the hundredth time, the column sank to a crouching position. At this rate they were never going to safely make it back to Fort Felix. The men were tiring. Constantly stopping and having to swap their burden for their weapons was starting to take a toll on their patience and energy. Corvo felt the frustration every bit as much as the men under his command. A few moments later Vortrix gave the all-clear signal, and the men resumed their journey.

"If my shoulder didn't ache so from carrying this bag, I would laugh," Flavius said quietly as he came alongside Corvo. "We must be a strange sight."

Corvo chuckled. "The cream of Rome's legions carrying baskets through a forest — no wonder the tribesmen tremble before us. I wonder what Caesar would think if he could see us now."

"Cream of the legions might be overstating it a bit, Marcus," said Flavius with a smile. "I think you forget in whose company we march. Besides, it could be worse."

"Really? How so?"

"My uncle was in one of the two legions Emperor Caligula sent to invade Britannia twenty or so years ago. I can recall him telling my father and I how the invasion was called off at the last moment, and the mad emperor instead sent the legions to collect sea shells to take back to Rome."

Corvo shot his friend a look. "That was just a story."

"Maybe, maybe not. My uncle stood by that story until the day he died. Besides, from what I've heard Caligula was mad enough to order such a thing."

Corvo nodded; that much was true.

"So you see, things could be worse. We could be carrying fir cones back to Fort Felix."

"Not sure what sort of reception we'd get from the legate and the others if we turned up with fir cones."

"One that included a lot of sharp steel, I would imagine," Flavius replied wryly.

Corvo groaned when Vortrix signalled for the column to stop again. "This is ridiculous. We will never get back at this rate. Here, look after my basket while I go and speak to our Gaulish friend and try to impress on him the need for speed as well as caution." Glad to be free of the weight of the basket he was carrying, Corvo crept silently up to Vortrix's side. "What is it this time?" He had tried to hide the irritation in his voice, but Vortrix's expression suggested that he had failed.

"I can get us back safely at my pace or I can go quicker, in which case I cannot guarantee that we won't run into their war band."

Corvo took a deep breath and closed his eyes, trying to control his exasperation. "No, do what you must, but understand that every time you bring us to a halt, it gives the war band a little longer to close in on our position. Anyway, why did you halt us this time?"

"I heard movement in the undergrowth."

"Where?"

Vortrix nodded and Corvo turned in the direction the Gaul indicated just as a large stag stepped out from its concealed position, chewing a mouthful of leaves. It stared in their direction, as if assessing whether they were a threat, and then calmly walked off into the trees to their right.

"A stag this time, Centurion — next time it might be a Germani scout."

Corvo took his point. He patted the Gaul on the shoulder and resumed his position next to Flavius, picking up his basket of coins as he did so.

"Anything?" asked Flavius.

"A stag. A big one too. Vortrix is cautious, but rightly so. I just wish I knew where the war band was."

"Now, where's the fun in that?" Flavius grinned. "Mind you, venison for dinner would have been nice tonight." Ahead of them, Vortrix gave the signal to advance.

When Corvo judged that they were perhaps halfway back to Fort Felix, against his better judgment, he joined Vortrix up front and told him they needed to take a short rest so the men could get a drink and ease their aching arms and shoulders. Vortrix nodded, and a couple of hundred paces on they came across a small clearing. Corvo gave the order to rest but remain vigilant.

"I don't remember seeing this clearing on the way to the enemy camp," Corvo said to Vortrix.

"That is because you asked me to take us back to Fort Felix by the most direct route, not the way we came. I have taken us on a slight detour in case they left more lookouts. It will not prolong our journey by too much."

"And exactly how much farther do we have left?"

"Your instincts are good, Centurion. I would estimate that we are about halfway home."

"All right, but from now on take the most direct route. The men are tiring, and we have no idea where the war band is."

"As you wish."

Just then, Atilus came over to Corvo looking worried.

"What is it, Atilus?"

"You'd better come and see this, Centurion," said the former gladiator evasively.

Corvo sighed and followed Atilus as he strode into the trees on the edge of the small clearing.

"Where are you going, Atilus? I gave orders for nobody to leave the clearing."

Atilus said nothing and just led Corvo a little deeper into the trees. Corvo was going to order him to stop and tell him what was going on when Atilus came to a halt and then stepped aside to give him a better view. A log, suspended by vine ropes at either end, swayed gently back and forth in front of them. In the middle of the log was a dark red stain that dripped on the ground beneath it. A few paces away lay the body of a legionary. Corvo could not see who it was, as his head had been reduced to little more than pulp, such had been the force of the impact. Corvo struggled to keep down the meagre contents of his stomach.

"He wandered off to take a piss and must have triggered their trap."

"Who was it?" asked Corvo.

"Hortix."

Corvo thought for a few moments until he could recall the man's face. He had been a slave they had bought on the march from Rome to Brundisium at the very beginning of their mission. He had proved to be loyal, brave and a quick learner.

"Damn it to Hades! Nobody else leaves the clearing. If there's one trap, there's likely to be more," said Corvo. With a last look at the man's ruined face, Corvo turned and hurried back to camp, where after gathering the men together, he told them what had happened. "Nobody wanders off, and certainly not alone. Felix, do you think you can manage the coins Hortix was carrying as well as your own?" Felix nodded. "Excellent. Then let's be on our way. The sooner we're out of this damned forest and safely behind Felix's walls, the better."

The men issued a collective groan as they picked up their burdens and fell into line again. Corvo glanced at the leaden sky and estimated it to be perhaps mid-afternoon. He hoped that they would be clear of the forest before it started to get dark, as their chances of spotting traps then would be non-existent.

They hadn't been walking for long when Vortrix gave the signal to halt yet again, then furiously gestured for Corvo to join him. Placing his basket of coins on the ground, Corvo hurried forward to where the Gaul stood waiting for him.

"What is it this time, Vortrix? Another stag?" The Gaul pointed and Corvo followed his gesture. "Dear Mithras!" Corvo stared at the grisly sight before him. Then, when he had managed to fully absorb what he was looking at, he slowly approached.

Tied to a large tree was a naked man. His arms had been outstretched and tied to branches on either side of him, and he had also been secured to the tree by a vine tied around his neck so that he could not move his head. His legs had been broken and hung limply at strange angles. One ear had been sliced off and both eyes had been savagely gouged out. None of this had killed him, however, and had merely been carried out for sadistic pleasure. When his captors had tired of toying with him, they had sliced a cross in his belly, from which his innards had slipped out to coil on the forest floor beneath him. His passing had been long and painful.

"Do you recognise him, Centurion?"

Vortrix's words made Corvo start. He had been so preoccupied by the horrendous sight that he had all but forgotten about the man standing next to him.

"What? Yes … yes, it's Milo, one of the three men who escaped us back at the tribe's camp. One of Traianus' men."

"Then I will not mourn him."

"No man deserves to die like that. These tribes are nothing but barbarians." He felt Vortrix bristle beside him, aware that the Gauls were considered nothing but barbarians themselves, even the ones who were Roman citizens.

"They betrayed us and killed Optio Nerva and others. Your grief is wasted on them, Centurion."

Corvo was about to reply when a rustling noise behind them drew their attention. Corvo reached for his gladius while Vortrix lowered his spear in readiness. Both relaxed when they saw Atilus and Flavius.

"Sorry, Marcus, I know you told us to wait, but you've been gone some time. We were worried that you'd fallen foul of one of their traps and… By all the gods…" Flavius' gaze had fallen on the body. "Is that Milo?"

"What remains of him, yes," replied Corvo.

"Is there no end to their savagery?"

"Is this the work of the war band, Vortrix?" asked Corvo.

Vortrix shook his head. "No, there are few tracks, and if the war band were in the area we would have run into them by now. The man has not been dead long. This is the work of a small group with time on their hands."

"So a patrol then?"

"Most likely, or men left to keep watch."

"Which means they could still be around here."

"I would almost…" Before Vortrix could complete his sentence, a cluster of warriors came screaming out from behind trees and bushes and rushed the four men. By the time Corvo and Flavius had drawn their gladii, Atilus had already killed one with a powerful thrust of his sword and sent another tumbling to the ground. Vortrix had also killed the warrior who came screaming towards him, his axe raised to cleave the Gaul's head in two. Vortrix had merely taken a couple of paces back, angled his spear downwards and tripped the warrior up. As the man had tried to struggle back to his feet, he had thrust his spear deep into the man's chest.

Two warriors had squared off against both Corvo and Flavius. Although the tribesmen still outnumbered the Romans, they were unable to make their superior numbers count due to the proximity of the trees.

One of the tribesmen facing Corvo swung wildly towards Corvo's neck with his sword, but Corvo was able to easily deflect the stroke with his gladius before quickly stepping back to avoid the thrust from the second warrior. The first warrior came in again with two quick strokes, both of which Corvo managed to block, though he was silently cursing himself for having left his shield back in the clearing.

To his right, Flavius caught a glancing blow on his forearm, but killed the man who had inflicted the wound when he over-extended and left himself vulnerable. To his right Atilus and

Vortrix were involved in their own life or death struggle with a warrior each.

Corvo was oblivious to everything going on around him. His world had shrunk to the ground in front of him and the two men who filled it. Cut, thrust, parry, feint. Corvo was managing to hold them at bay but had not as yet managed to go on the offensive. One of the warriors, a man in his late twenties with a livid scar down his right cheek, swung wildly for Corvo's head again, but this time instead of trying to deflect the stroke, Corvo ducked under it and stepped forward. As he did so, he thrust his gladius and was rewarded with a cry of pain as his blade pierced the warrior's stomach. Corvo had deliberately put all his weight behind the thrust so that his momentum sent him stumbling into the warrior he had stabbed and away from the downward slice of the second warrior's sword, which he felt cut through the air behind him. Corvo pulled his gladius free and turned to face the second warrior, who had also recovered his balance. He began to close in on Corvo.

Shouts from behind Corvo drifted through the trees and the warrior facing Corvo hesitated, distracted by the noise. Corvo seized his moment and raised his gladius, as if he were going to chop down into the warrior's neck. The startled warrior instinctively raised his own sword to block the blow, but Corvo's move had been a feint and instead he altered the angle of his stroke and brought it down in an arc which sliced across the warrior's exposed stomach. It was not a killing blow, but it was enough to disorientate the warrior. Before he could recover, Corvo stabbed the blade into the man's side with a backhanded thrust, then quickly withdrew it. The warrior dropped his sword and then collapsed face-first onto the muddy forest floor.

Corvo spun round to meet the next warrior, but instead he found a dozen of his men with gladii and shields at the ready, led by Batilus. They had come running the moment they heard the tell-tale sound of steel on steel, but they had not been needed. All eight of the warriors who had attacked them lay dead on the ground.

"What took you so long, Centurion?" said Atilus, grinning. "We were getting bored waiting." Flavius and Vortrix were also grinning, enjoying the centurion's discomfort.

"That's because I was the only one facing real warriors. You three had nothing but children and old men to face," Corvo retorted, though as he glanced around at the bodies littering the ground, he knew that not to be true.

Corvo suddenly noticed the shocked look on Batilus' face and that of the men with him. He turned and realised that they were staring at the gruesome remains of Milo, still tied to the tree.

"He has been avenged," said Corvo, looking at Batilus. "But have a good look at him, men, because that is the fate that awaits us all if we get caught."

"Nothing more than the traitor deserved," said Batilus, full of contempt. "It's a pity it wasn't Traianus." He spat on the ground in front of the mutilated body and then turned to walk back to the clearing, followed by the others.

"Not one for forgiveness, is he?" said Flavius wryly.

"I don't blame him." Corvo took one last look at Milo's body and then followed Batilus back to the clearing.

They arrived at the edge of the clearing in which Fort Felix stood late that afternoon. The dark clouds threatened yet more rain and were chasing away the pale daylight much earlier than usual. From their position just inside the treeline, they could hear Roman voices bellowing orders from within the fort.

"Sounds like Centurion Galba keeping the men on their toes," said Corvo, smiling.

"At least we know the fort is still in our hands," replied Flavius.

"But not the others, it seems," said Atilus. He gestured towards the west, where above the trees there was a pall of dark grey smoke snaking into the sky.

"Fort Otto?" asked Flavius.

"I should think so," said Corvo. "My guess is that Duma will face the same fate when the tribesmen find that is also empty, if it hasn't already."

"Let's hope that the plan worked and both garrisons made it safely to Felix," said Atilus.

A rustling from the foliage to their right drew their attention and a few moments later Vortrix appeared, looking bemused at the expressions on the other men's faces.

"Were you expecting someone else?"

Corvo chose not to take the bait. "Anything?" he asked.

"No," said the Gaul, sounding disappointed, "the immediate area is clear. We should have no trouble crossing the clearing to Fort Felix."

"Finally the gods smile on us," said Corvo ruefully.

"More likely they're just playing with us," countered Flavius.

"So long as they let us get safely across with our cargo, I'll happily take it. Get the men on their feet, Lucius. It's time to be on our way."

Almost immediately after emerging from the treeline, they could hear the anxious shouts of centurions and optios coming from within the fort as they berated the men for moving too slowly to their positions on the fort's ramparts. This time as they approached the fort, Corvo and his men were soon identified and the order to stand down was issued. When they were no more than fifty paces from the fort, its huge wooden gates were swung open and Corvo and his exhausted men struggled in as quickly as they were able. The gates were slammed shut the moment the last man was inside.

The fort was a hive of activity with legionaries busy undertaking various tasks in the square, on the ramparts and around the storerooms. There were now nearly three times as many men stationed there than there had been early that morning, and Corvo was glad that having to sort out the living arrangements for so many new men was not his responsibility. At least he hoped it wasn't.

"Centurion Corvo, welcome back."

Corvo looked up from where he stood doubled over, trying to catch his breath, to see Legate Crispus, his son Gaius, Centurion Galba and Tribune Ortius looking at him with bemused expressions.

"Legate. Men," replied Corvo between huge gulps of air while forcing himself to stand straight, even if his shoulders protested vehemently.

"Your mission was a success, I see," said the legate, eyeing the bags and baskets of silver coins lying at the feet of Corvo's men.

"It was, Legate."

"And eventful?" asked the legate, raising a knowing eyebrow.

"You could say that, Legate, yes."

"You seem to be considerably fewer than when you left."

"I regret to report that our losses are grievous."

The legate nodded. "Well, let's get this silver somewhere safe. You and your men should have something to eat, Centurion, and then we'll have an officers' meeting. Something tells me that your story is going to be most engaging."

"Food, drink and a new pair of shoulders would be most welcome, Legate," said Corvo, smiling.

"Well, I can certainly help you with the first two, but you're on your own for new body parts. Follow me — I'll show you where I want the silver stored." The legate turned and started to make his way towards the main storeroom within the camp.

Less than half an hour later, the silver was stacked in what the legate had deemed the safest place in the fort, and the legate's son, an optio and a couple of legionaries were busy counting and recording it all in ledgers.

Corvo had then joined his men in the mess hall for the first hot meal he had enjoyed in what felt like forever. Tiredness was starting to overwhelm him, and he craved his bunk, sure he could sleep for a full day and night. Any such thoughts were dashed when a legionary he didn't recognise came to inform him that the officers were gathered, awaiting his arrival to begin the debrief.

Corvo sighed, downed the last of his watered wine and followed the man out. Sleep it seemed, was going to have to wait.

CHAPTER 10

The legate absentmindedly scratched his cheek as Corvo finished his debrief regarding their mission. When it was clear that Corvo had nothing more to add, the legate reached for the wineskin, poured himself another cup and then offered it round. He took a long sip and leant back in his rickety wooden chair.

"You've done damn well, Centurion, damn well." The legate was beaming. "Gaius believes you recovered…" He looked at his son.

"About nine tenths."

"Yes, about nine tenths of what should have been there," said the legate. "The portion that was missing has probably been handed out to the chieftain's men to buy their loyalty."

Corvo nodded while also wondering how much of it was actually sitting in the pockets of his own men.

"It doesn't matter too much anyway, as some of the chieftain's own treasures were also stored with the silver, so our losses are negligible. The men are going to be happy tomorrow, and not before time."

"Is morale no better?" asked Corvo.

"Worse, though consolidating our forces in one place seems to have lifted their spirits, and knowing that they no longer have to go out on search patrols will help. Nothing raises morale, though, like a palm full of silver."

"It was at some cost, though, Legate."

"True, but acceptable," the legate countered. Corvo thought of Optio Nerva lying dead in the mud with a slit throat and wasn't sure if he agreed with the legate's assessment. "So Traianus and his men are gone?"

"Most are dead. Some remained loyal to me. Three escaped, including Traianus, but we found one of them not far from here."

"Ah, yes, the one who had been tortured. And where do you think Traianus and the other one are?"

"Dead, probably. The forests are filled with tribesmen — it's hard to imagine how they would manage to evade them."

"And then there are the traps?"

"Yes, sir. One of our men wandered off and triggered a trap — a log strung up by vines that comes hurtling down and crushes the body, or in this case head, of the one who set it off. They're not going to kill many men that way, but they certainly set the men's nerves on edge and spread terror. If they're looking at the ground for fear of setting off a trap, they're not watching the trees, and they become more vulnerable to a surprise attack."

"And you think there are more of them out there?"

"I think it would be prudent to assume so, sir, yes."

"Let us hope that you are right about Traianus. With him gone, Batilus and his men should calm down, don't you think, Tribune Ortius?"

"Batilus knows how to hold a grudge. I don't suppose he will be entirely satisfied until Traianus' dead body is lying at his feet. That said, news that most of Traianus' men are dead coupled with the arrival of the silver should see a marked improvement in his attitude. Where Batilus leads, others follow."

"He fought well and gave me no problems on our mission," offered Corvo. "Beneath the attitude lies a capable soldier."

The legate nodded. "That is good. It is a shame about Optio Nerva, though. Men like him are the backbone of the legions."

The cluster of officers around the legate's table all nodded.

"To Sextus Nerva," said Galba, raising his cup, and they all echoed him.

"Now, to matters at hand. As you will no doubt have deduced, the plan to evacuate Forts Duma and Otto and draw the tribesmen away from their camp worked well," said the legate. "Instead of splitting his forces, their chieftain appears to have led his entire war band to Fort Otto, but by the time they got there, Tribune Ortius had already withdrawn his forces and was marching here. By the time the war band arrived at Otto, all they would have found is an empty fort containing nothing of use to them. Meanwhile, Centurion Jovian had also led his men from Fort Duma to here without incident."

"Didn't see a single one of those hairy-backed bastards. Begging your pardon, sir," Jovian added sheepishly.

The legate just smiled. "If what you say is true, Centurion Corvo, then while at Fort Otto, the chieftain will likely have received news from one of his sons that his wife was raped, his other son killed, and his camp raided. I agree with you that in a blind rage he will in all likelihood have hurried straight back to his camp rather than try and cut you off, which is why you were able to get back here reasonably untroubled. I can only imagine the rage the man is in right now." The legate took another mouthful of wine. "It's a shame that he set fire to Fort Otto, but it can't be helped."

"But Traianus, curse his name, has made life more difficult for us by killing and shaming the chieftain's family," said Corvo ruefully.

"True. There is no chance that they will be prepared to negotiate a peace now. But had Traianus not done what he did, the chieftain may not have reacted the way he did and your head and those of your men might well be adorning his hut by now. Take a win when one is given, Centurion, even if there are conditions."

"Yes, sir."

"So what happens now, sir?" asked Tribune Ortius.

"Now we wait. The next move, I suspect, is down to their chieftain. I have all the men under my command in one place and we have recovered the silver, meaning that both our men and Centurion Corvo's men can be paid, though it will do them no good out here in the middle of nowhere. Other than that, things have not changed. The men across the Rhenus will still not come to our aid, and I have not received any orders to retreat. In fact, I've received no orders at all, which just reinforces my belief that I was sent here to wither and die, both politically and physically. I intend to do neither."

Corvo was nodding in agreement when suddenly he realised what had been troubling him. "Sir, where is Arus?"

"I wondered when you were going to notice that the old fox was missing. I've sent him on a separate mission to the forts on the other side of the Rhenus."

"On his own?" asked Corvo, suddenly alarmed.

"Calm down, Centurion. Legionary Gemmellus has gone with him to make sure that he doesn't get lost. Besides, I don't think you give the man enough credit — he is more than capable of finding his way safely across the Rhenus."

"Of course, sir. Sorry. May I ask what his mission is?"

"To try and persuade, by fair means or foul, Helvius and Scipio to let the rest of my legion accompany him back over the Rhenus. If he can do that and we put down this tribal uprising, it will scupper the emperor's plans for me, and he might be minded to just let me slip off into retirement somewhere out of the way. Arus was also going to send riders to Rome to see what he can learn. He has more contacts than I and may find out what is really going on. At the very least he may come back with fresh orders. I sent my own riders weeks ago, but none have yet returned. Perhaps he will fare better."

"The emperor is just as likely to send an assassin, sir," said Tribune Ortius.

"Every officer who has enjoyed a modicum of success lives with that threat, Tribune. Besides, it's the only play I have. Now, the hour is late, and I am sure that Centurion Corvo and his men are exhausted, so I think we will finish there, men. Thank you. We will parade the men tomorrow morning and offer them their pay. Those that don't want to keep it about their person can rest assured that it will be kept as safe as possible under guard in what I have designated the strong room. Once we have done that, all officers will accompany me on a tour of the fort's defences. We have worked hard today, and Centurion Galba's input has been invaluable, but I suspect there are still many things we could do to strengthen our defences. I would be grateful to hear your opinions, especially yours, Centurion Corvo, since you went through something similar in Armenia. Right, dismissed, men. Sleep well, and thank you again."

The officers all bade the legate a good night, saluted and then left the room to seek out their bunks.

Corvo was asleep within moments of laying down his head.

The night passed all too quickly, and he was still asleep when he felt a hand shake his shoulder.

"Marcus!"

Corvo ignored the call and refused to open his eyes.

"Marcus!" The shake was more insistent this time and showed no sign of abating.

"What? Can't you see that I'm asleep?"

"You can have a go at me later, if we're both still here, but in the meantime I suggest you get up and out on the double. We've got company."

Corvo's eyes were open in a moment, and in one fluid movement he had sat up and swung his legs off his bunk. Flavius stood in front of him, holding his helmet and gladius. "What's happening, Lucius?"

"The tribesmen are here."

Corvo leapt to his feet, snatching his helmet and gladius from his friend. After strapping on his sword belt, he slipped his helmet on and then grabbed his chest armour, which he began to fasten as they moved out of the door. Outside, the fort was a flurry of activity as men rushed backwards and forwards across the square, some in the same state of undress as Corvo. Centurions Galba and Jovian were barking orders at anybody and everybody. When his armour was fitted and he felt at least half presentable, Corvo scanned the fort for the legate and found him standing on the rampart above the gates, his son and Tribune Ortius next to him. Corvo adjusted his helmet strap and then began to make his way across the square to the steps leading up to the northern rampart, legionaries rushing past him in both directions carrying javelins and arrows.

"Legate," said Corvo coming to attention and saluting. "Tribunes," he then added, addressing Tribunes Crispus and Ortius.

"Ah, Centurion Corvo. I trust you slept well?" the legate greeted.

"Thank you, Legate. I did," said Corvo, turning to look out over the clearing.

"Good. Well, as you can see our hairy friends have decided to pay us a visit."

Corvo stared at the distant treeline, in front of which stood a deep throng of warriors, snarling and shouting insults at the Romans.

"How many of them are there, would you say?"

Corvo studied their lines, but men seemed to be disappearing in and out of the trees, making it almost impossible to assess their strength. He wondered if that was their intention, to disguise their true numbers from the Romans.

"Difficult to say, Legate. Five hundred at least, I would estimate."

"More, I think, but as you say, there's no way to know for certain."

"Will they attack?" asked Tribune Ortius.

"Oh, yes. But not just yet," replied the legate.

"And why is that?"

"Because before men can hurl themselves at a fortified position knowing that they are going to be assailed by a storm of arrows and javelins, they need to first work up the courage. They will shout and threaten, drink themselves brave and only then will they attack," Corvo replied. "Then the butchery will commence."

Footsteps behind them drew their attention, and Centurion Galba saluted. "The men are dispersed as we practised, Legate."

"Excellent, thank you, Centurion Galba." The legate turned his gaze back out to the clearing and the tribesmen positioned on the other side. Something was happening. A few moments later, a cluster of men stepped forward from the mass of tribesmen, bringing with them four horses. Two of the men were dragging somebody between them.

"It looks like our guests have laid on some entertainment for us," said the legate. The officers all stepped up to the parapet for a better look.

"That's one of ours," said Tribune Ortius as they watched the tribesmen throw a man to the ground. To stop him trying to get up and run, one of the tribesmen placed his foot on the man's stomach to hold him in place. Meanwhile, another of the Germani, a big man with long blond hair tied in a bunch to the side of his head and with a long and wild beard, stepped forward a few more paces.

"Anybody recognise our man?" asked the legate.

Most shook their heads. "If I had to guess, I would say that it's either Traianus or his companion," said Corvo. "They've made such a mess of him already that it's hard to see clearly."

They all watched helplessly as the tribesmen tied each of the prisoner's arms to a different horse and then repeated the procedure with his legs. The horses were gently coaxed forward until the man found himself suspended in midair. The prisoner began to scream and wail in terror.

Corvo quickly turned and began to look along the ramparts until his gaze settled on the man he was searching for. "Kochar! Here, at the double."

The Syrian archer, one of two brothers who had joined Corvo on his mission to Armenia, his brother having been killed, hurried across to where Corvo was standing with the other officers.

"Do you think you can hit him, Kochar?"

"Their chieftain?" asked Kochar, looking at the large blond warrior several paces in front of the rest.

"No, our man. Do you think you can hit him before they tear him apart?"

Kochar wet a finger and held it up, assessing the wind direction. Then he looked long and hard at where the Roman prisoner was screaming in agony as first the front two horses were urged forward and then the rear two, pulling the ropes ever tauter.

Kochar shook his head. "I am sorry, Centurion; if there was no wind, perhaps, but with the wind as it is, no. Their chieftain, however…"

Corvo glanced at the legate, but he merely shook his head. "No. All right, Kochar, thank you. You may return to your position."

The Syrian nodded, then turned and left.

"It was a nice idea, Centurion, but I'm afraid we're all just going to have to ride this particular horror out," said the legate.

The man's screams were horrific as the horses pulled further apart, the tension in the ropes increasing all the time. The more he screamed, the louder the Germani warriors watching behind him cheered.

Corvo desperately wanted to look away but refused to give in to his emotions. Regardless of whether that was Traianus or his comrade Albinius out there, neither deserved such a horrific death. Whatever they had become, they had once been Roman soldiers, and no Roman soldier should die such an ignominious death.

The man gave one last high-pitched scream and suddenly all four horses stumbled forward as the tension in the ropes gave way, their handlers struggling to get them back under control as the smell of blood spooked them. The prisoner's head and torso dropped to the ground while a limb remained tied to the rope trailing behind each horse. The horde of warriors in front of the treeline roared their approval. As some of the warriors led the jittery horses away into the trees, the chieftain who had not watched the execution and had instead stared rigidly at the ramparts above the gate, turned and slowly walked to where the mangled torso lay. Then, with his back to the fort, he raised his war axe and brought it down in a powerful blow. He then bent down and holding it by the hair, he lifted the man's head into the air to the raucous approval of his warriors. When their cheering began to settle, he then turned and walked to what he considered to be just out of bow shot and held the head aloft, so everyone on the ramparts could see it. With a mighty grunt, he then threw the head as hard as he could towards the fort's gates before turning and walking slowly back towards his warriors.

The Roman walls were still, the brutality of what they had just watched shocking the men who manned the ramparts into silence.

"Now, Centurion Jovian!" the legate suddenly roared, startling Corvo and those around him. Moments later, the unmistakeable sound of a scorpio being fired filled the air. Across the clearing the tribesmen roared in panic as the bolt punched clean through two men and into a tree behind them, leaving them pinned against the trunk. Fearing more projectiles were heading their way, the tribesmen quickly melted into the trees behind them and out of sight.

"Good shot, Centurion!" called the legate. Centurion Jovian merely nodded.

"I didn't know we had one of those at our disposal," said Corvo as he dragged his gaze away from the sight of the two warriors pinned helplessly to the tree. He couldn't see from that distance whether they were dead, but if they weren't they soon would be, as the bolt from a scorpio left a huge hole in whatever it struck.

"Two, actually," replied the legate cheerily. "Found them when we were preparing the defences earlier. Needed a bit of maintenance, but now they're as good as new, as you've just seen."

"I don't suppose you found any ballista while you were looking around, did you?" asked Corvo.

"Sadly, Centurion, two scorpiones and a limited number of bolts is all we found, but it's more than you thought we had to start with."

Corvo nodded. "Then we will have to make do."

"That's the spirit. I suspect that once our German friends have got over the shock of seeing two of their comrades knocked off their feet and pinned to a tree, they'll be back to have a go at us. I have allocated you and what remains of your men to the rampart on the left of the gate, Centurion." Corvo smiled, confusing the legate. "Have I said something funny, Centurion?"

"Apologies, Legate — no, you haven't. I'm smiling because it was the same position I occupied when we defended Fort Lipa back in Armenia."

"Ah, I see. Well, let's hope you are as successful at holding this wall as you were that one. I suggest that we keep the men stood-to for a while longer and if the tribesmen haven't come back by then, we'll rotate the men, half on and half off. Everybody agree?" The officers all nodded. "Then let's be about it, men." They all saluted the legate and then hurried off to their command positions.

CHAPTER 11

The tribesmen came back just a short while before Corvo was preparing to stand half his men down. It started as a gentle thumping coming from somewhere in the forest, a thumping which grew louder and louder, eventually sending scores of crows into a panicked flight from their nests high in the trees. When the first of the warriors emerged from the tree cover, Corvo could see that the noise had been caused by the warriors banging on their shields with their axe and spear shafts. Once they were clear of the trees, the warriors began to roar and shout until all the Romans could hear from their positions on the ramparts was an indecipherable wall of noise.

The Romans watched them impassively and without a sound. Most had witnessed this sort of behaviour before and knew that while it was meant to intimidate them, it was mostly to help the warriors work up the courage to attack. Every now and then, urged on by the others, one of the warriors would dash a few strides farther forward than his comrades and would hurl insults and threats at the watching Romans, before eventually running out of vitriol and resuming his position back in the host.

One warrior dashed forward, turned his back on the Romans, dropped his breeches and bent over, much to the amusement of his fellow warriors.

"Permission to use the scorpio to try and impale him, Centurion," said Galba from Corvo's left.

"Tempting, I grant you, Titus, but perhaps not the best use of our limited ammunition," replied Corvo, smiling.

"Probably not, but it would have shut him up."

Having pulled his breeches back up, the warrior walked back to his friends. Another barrage of roars and shouts carried across the clearing before yet another warrior stepped forward. He came to a stop next to the headless torso of the Roman they had pulled apart earlier and proceeded to urinate on him, accompanied by howls of laughter from his comrades. Then he too rejoined the ranks.

Gradually the shouting and banging began to die off until an eerie silence settled over the clearing and both sides stood staring at one another. After a few moments, the tall blond man who the Romans had assumed was the chieftain stepped through the throng to take up a position a few strides in front of his men. He spent a few moments staring at the fort and then raised his axe high in the air, bellowing something that only his men understood. A few moments later, his men issued a mighty roar and then surged towards the fort. As Corvo watched a steady stream of warriors emerge from the tree cover, he decided that his estimate of five hundred had been well short of the mark.

There was no order to the tribesmen's attack; their warriors just charged en masse, the fittest and fastest racing ahead of their comrades, eager to claim the glory. The Romans stood stoically above them, waiting. When the first tribesmen were a little over two hundred paces away, Corvo heard the twang of the scorpio again, except this time there were two. He watched the first bolt slam into a warrior's chest, knocking him off his feet and sending him flying through the air until he collided with two more warriors and sent them crashing to the ground under him. The other bolt had struck a warrior in the head, disintegrating it in a red mist before flying on and slamming into another warrior's stomach, killing him instantly. Like the tribesmen's traps, they were not weapons designed to kill many of the enemy. Instead, their purpose was to instil fear and panic.

To his right, Corvo could hear Centurion Jovian barking at his men to be quicker about loading the artillery.

The warriors were about a hundred and twenty paces from the fort's walls when Tribune Ortius ordered, "Loose!"

Scores of arrows flew into the air before dropping into the mass of warriors bearing down on the fort.

A legionary to Corvo's right cried out and stumbled backwards, an arrow in his throat. Another to his left suffered a similar fate, although he was struck in the right eye.

Another volley of arrows arced into the sky and dropped among the attacking warriors, but not as many found a target this time.

"Javelins!" shouted Corvo. Along the ramparts dozens of legionaries hefted their pilums, and when Corvo judged the enemy to be no more than forty strides away, he gave the order to throw. The deadly hail of iron-tipped barbs tore into the tribesmen, thinning their numbers considerably.

The Germani had massed their own archers behind the attacking warriors, and a volley of arrows flew towards the ramparts in response.

"Get your shields up! Get your shields up!" Corvo bellowed, leading by example. He felt his shield vibrate as two arrows thudded into it. Others had not been so quick, and several men lay dead or wounded along the ramparts either side of Corvo.

Corvo watched as one legionary to his right lowered his shield and looked wide-eyed at the three arrows stuck in it. He saw the centurion watching and grinned. "I've always been lucky, sir."

Corvo was about to berate the young soldier for lowering his shield when right before his eyes a spear struck the legionary in the neck with such force that it passed clean through. He looked at Corvo in disbelief and then stumbled from the ramparts to the ground below.

There was no time for Corvo to dwell on what he had just witnessed as at various points along the ramparts, tribesmen were now scaling the walls, either with grappling ropes or with the help of rudimentary ladders. At the moment the legionaries were holding them off, their numbers sufficient to repel the tribesmen who had safely made it to the fort's walls and were now attempting to breach its sanctum.

The scorpiones fired again and although he never saw them strike home, Corvo knew that their crews couldn't miss, given the masses of men below. The bolts would have carved a bloody mess through whatever they struck.

A cry from behind him alerted Corvo, and he spun just in time to see a legionary driven to the ground by a large warrior who had managed to safely scale a ladder. He was now looming over the legionary, preparing to strike. Corvo rushed behind the man and thrust his gladius into his bare back, before kicking his body down into the square below. Corvo nodded at the legionary and stepped back. The legionary gratefully scrambled to his feet and went to tip the ladder over, but he found another warrior was already at the top and climbing onto the rampart. Before the legionary could react, the warrior smashed his small axe into the Roman's head, his helmet providing little protection.

Seeing the danger, Corvo rushed over and ran the man through before he could pull his axe free of the dead man's head. His body fell silently to the ground below, landing on some of his fellow tribesmen.

More ladders were appearing along the ramparts, quicker than the defenders could tip them over. Corvo rushed to the aid of Atilus, who was busily fighting off two warriors. One was already on the ramparts, the other was at the top of a ladder, trying to climb over while helping his comrade. Neither man saw Corvo coming, and he was easily able to thrust his gladius into the neck of the man at the top of the ladder. He fell silently backwards, taking the man immediately behind with him. Free from the worry of being stabbed in the back, Atilus hurled himself at the remaining warrior and was soon able to overpower him. A deep thrust into his belly brought the man to his knees before another stroke opened his throat.

From somewhere outside the fort, a horn sounded three long blasts and Corvo watched as the Germani warriors started to withdraw. For some, withdrawal was impossible. Those already caught up in individual combat were unable to extricate themselves and head for the ladders without leaving their backs exposed. Others were so caught up in the heat of battle that they had no intention of withdrawing. They had a foothold in the enemy fort and would either take it or die with glory. Corvo watched as one by one these men were brought down. Romans now free of their own battles rushed over to help beleaguered comrades, swinging the odds in their favour. It was not long before the ramparts were clear of living warriors, those lying wounded soon being put to the sword by the defenders.

Corvo glanced over the wall and saw a mass of tribesmen running back towards the treeline, the ground behind them strewn with their dead. It was not a panicked retreat, Corvo noticed, and the tribesmen had had the presence of mind to take most of their ladders with them. Those they didn't were quickly pulled up into the fort, where the enemy would be denied their use.

"First blood to us, I think, Centurion," said the legate as he came striding over.

Corvo glanced around at the ramparts and wasn't so sure. While there were undoubtedly more dead tribesmen than Romans, he didn't think he would describe it as a victory. The tribesmen were many and they were not. He didn't doubt that the chieftain was prepared to expend all of his warriors to avenge his wife and son.

"First blood, Legate, yes, but there is a lot more to be spilled before this is over, I think."

"Well, if they keep throwing themselves at our walls like that, we'll soon thin their numbers for them."

Corvo chose not to point out to the legate that the chieftain had only committed part of his force to the attack, yet they had still managed to breach the walls and gain a foothold on the ramparts. If next time the chieftain chose to commit all his strength, the Romans would probably be overwhelmed.

"I'll get some casualty figures, Legate," said Corvo.

"Thank you."

"Do you think they'll come again today, Centurion?" asked Tribune Crispus. It was telling that he addressed his question to Corvo and not his father.

Corvo glanced at the treeline into which the warriors had disappeared. The large blond warrior who they assumed was the chieftain was standing with four other men. Three of them were tall and blond like himself, but one was smaller with dark hair, although he was dressed like the others. The chieftain appeared to be having an intense argument with the dark-haired man.

"Centurion?"

"What? Oh yes, sorry. Yes, I think they probably will attack again later today. Right now they'll be licking their wounds and drinking to build courage and trying to come up with a better plan. The chieftain and his advisors seem to be arguing about that very point right now."

The legate and his son followed Corvo's gaze and saw the cluster of warriors standing and arguing, intermittently pointing at the fort.

"Maybe they'll do our job for us and tear themselves apart. In my experience barbarian warriors only follow a successful leader," said the legate. "I shall be in my quarters. Send for me immediately if and when they return." The legate turned and started to make his way towards the steps leading down to the square, careful not to tread on any of the fallen dead or wounded.

After watching the legate go, Corvo went to summon Optio Nerva to conduct a casualty report like he had during the siege in Armenia and only just stopped himself in time before shouting the dead man's name. Instead, he called for Optio Valus. Once he had given Valus his task, Corvo walked the length of the ramparts, checking on his men and their dwindling supply of arrows and javelins.

"It's like history repeating itself, is it not?" said Flavius as he hurried to catch up with his friend.

"It is. And like the last time we found ourselves in this situation, we are running out of javelins and arrows. If we cannot thin their numbers while they are outside the walls, we have little chance of doing so once they are inside."

"So what are you thinking? Should a party go and retrieve what they safely can from outside?" asked Flavius.

"I don't see that we have a choice."

"Centurion!" The shout had come from the rampart above the gate, and both men looked in that direction and saw Atilus pointing over the palisade towards the forest. "We've got movement."

Corvo glanced at Flavius. "Well, they're back quicker than I thought they would be. You, Legionary...?" said Corvo, turning and pointing at a soldier who was helping to clear the ramparts.

"Ratilius, sir."

"Legionary Ratilius. Go and fetch the legate. Tell him the enemy are back."

It was news to Ratilius, and he nervously glanced over the palisade. He nodded and then dashed off to carry out his orders.

"Come on, Lucius, follow me," said Corvo, and he and Flavius started to jog along the ramparts, jumping bodies where necessary, towards where Atilus was waiting for them. By the time that they reached him, there were perhaps thirty tribesmen forming a line just out of bowshot from the ramparts. Unusually for tribesmen, these were all bowmen. They fanned out a couple of strides apart so that the whole of the fort's front was covered. Corvo watched them for a while. No other warriors had emerged from the trees.

"They're back already?" a voice asked. Corvo turned to find a red-faced legate hurrying towards him from the top of the steps. "Thought I'd have a bit more peace than that. So what are they up to?" He eased past his officers and leant against the palisade. The top had been whittled into sharp points to make any attempt to climb over more difficult.

"About thirty bowmen appeared a short while ago and have taken up position just out of bow range. There's been no sign of movement from anywhere else."

"So what in Hades are they doing? They must know that if they're safely out of bow range, then we are too?"

"They know," replied Corvo.

Tribune Ortius and the legate's son had also wandered over to join them now and looked equally bemused by the tribesmen's behaviour.

"Then what is the point? Are they just there to watch us? Thirty men seems a little excessive."

"No, they've been put there for a specific purpose," said Corvo confidently.

Everyone turned to face Corvo.

"And that is?" asked the legate.

"They're there to stop us retrieving any javelins or arrows. These ramparts might be out of range, but the ground in front of the fort isn't. As soon as we send men out to try and retrieve some ordnance, they'll release a deadly volley of arrows. They know that we only have a limited supply of arrows and javelins and that once they're exhausted, there is nothing we can do to stop them reaching the walls. Sheer weight of numbers will then mean they will eventually prevail."

"So their chieftain is perhaps wiser than we thought."

"That or he's being advised by an outsider familiar with our method of warfare or who has been in a similar position himself."

"That seems unlikely," said the legate.

Corvo thought differently but decided against contradicting his superior officer, though he had his suspicions.

"We could dislodge them with the scorpiones," offered Tribune Crispus.

"It would be a waste of ammunition, Tribune," said Corvo. "They have deliberately spaced themselves apart in case we deploy them. Each bolt would only kill one man at a time, and that's if our aim is true enough. They are better used when they attack in mass waves — the men are easier to hit and there's a greater chance of multiple casualties. No, they've thought this through."

"What if we try and retrieve the javelins at night? Perhaps we would have better luck then," offered Tribune Ortius.

"Only if we extinguish all torches and make it as dark as possible out there."

"But then we run the risk of hundreds of tribesmen closing in on the fort unseen and killing our foragers, or worse still, rushing our gates," added the legate.

"Quite," said Corvo.

"Then we will have to make do with what we have and improvise," said Tribune Crispus.

"I'm afraid so," confirmed Corvo.

"So be it. I'm going back to my quarters, but if anything changes, let me know." The legate turned to leave and nearly stumbled over a dead legionary's body. "And get more men clearing these ramparts." Shaking his head, the legate turned and headed towards his quarters, passing Centurion Galba on the way.

"Titus. Your timing is excellent. I want to resume my inspection of the ramparts, so can you get men clearing the bodies? Throw theirs over the walls, and arrange for ours to be cremated once a list of their names has been compiled. Strip everything useful off all the bodies. Maintain enough sentries, but also try to stand as many of the men down as possible. Get Centurion Jovian to help you, if he's finished playing with the scorpiones. Also, chase Valus up for that casualty report."

Galba nodded, saluted and then marched away, barking orders at anybody who caught his eye.

"Where do you want me, Marcus?" asked Flavius.

"You stay right here and be officer of the watch. If anything changes, send for me and the legate. I shouldn't be long carrying out my inspection."

CHAPTER 12

The tribesmen came again late that afternoon. Corvo had just started to think that he had perhaps been wrong, and they weren't going to show again that day, when the first cries went up from the forward sentries. Moments later hundreds of warriors emerged from the trees, roaring their defiance and hatred of the Romans. As Corvo rushed to assume his position on the north rampart again, he was aware of the hive of activity around him as hundreds of men raced to man their own positions.

"Not as many of them this time, I see," said the legate brightly as he came to stand next to Corvo and adjusted his helmet strap. But even as he spoke, to the west and the east more warriors emerged from the trees, forming three separate bodies of men. "Looks like I spoke too soon. They're going to hit us from three sides at once. Gaius, Tribune Ortius, each of you take one man in three from the north wall and reinforce the western and eastern ramparts. I don't care who takes which. Were the javelins and arrows evenly distributed along all three walls, Centurion?"

"No, Legate, most were left on the north wall where we expected the bulk of their army to attack," replied Corvo.

"Very well. Take a third of the javelins each but leave the arrows. I'm going to concentrate our archers above the gate. Optio Flavius!"

"Sir," said Flavius, coming to attention.

"I'd like you to take command of them, if you please."

"At once," replied Flavius and after nodding at Corvo, he ran off, barking orders for every archer to join him on the rampart above the gate, bringing with them every arrow they could find.

"We have to dominate them somewhere and I would like it to be here, where their chieftain can watch. If he sees that they are taking a mauling here, he may assume a similar thing is happening elsewhere and be minded to call a retreat. But only if we can bleed them enough here, at our gates. I have instructed Centurion Galba to command the strategic reserve with orders to act independently wherever and whenever he sees a threat; I trust his judgement." The legate noticed Corvo was smiling. "Have I said something that amuses you, Centurion, or is this another Armenian reminiscence?"

"The latter, sir. I left Centurion Galba in charge of the reserve back in Armenia. He wasn't too pleased to be missing out on the action and let me know it in no uncertain terms."

"Yes, well, it's fair to say he wasn't delighted this time either, but he had the good sense to not complain too much, given my rank. Fight well, Centurion. Courage and honour."

"Courage and honour, Legate."

A huge roar went up from the tribesmen, and both Corvo and the legate turned just in time to see all three groups of warriors race towards the fort. Behind them the bowmen walked slowly forward and began to shoot arrows at the ramparts.

"All right, here they come," said Corvo, taking a position in the middle of the men he was to command. "All we have to do is stop them getting onto the ramparts. Fight for your life and for the man either side of you. Fight for Rome!"

The men cheered and then started to hunker down behind their shields as the German archers came into range and began to pepper the ramparts. Flavius immediately gave the command to return fire. Hoping that the steady stream of arrows from above the gate would either be enough to divert the German archers' attention or even drive them back, Corvo gave the order to stand and prepare to throw javelins. He waited for the tribesmen to condense at the foot of the wall, their eagerness to be the first to climb the walls clouding their common sense, and then gave the order.

"Loose."

Scores of javelins thrown from just feet above the tribesmen tore into their ranks. From that range and with that trajectory, they were nearly all going to be killing throws.

"Again. Loose."

Corvo cursed when he realised that this time only half the men had a javelin to throw, though some of his men were improvising and throwing rocks and masonry instead. The tribesmen had noticed that the number of javelins had dwindled too and renewed their assault with vigour.

A legionary to Corvo's left dropped his gladius and clutched at his throat, from where an arrow now protruded. He stumbled forward and over the palisade, landing on several tribesmen below. Another legionary further along staggered backwards as an arrow took him in the left shoulder. He stood there motionless for a few moments and was then struck in the chest by a spear thrown by a warrior at the top of a ladder. The legionary stumbled backwards, dead long before his body hit the ground below.

Corvo raced over and thrust his gladius into the attacker's neck before then using his left foot to push the man backwards and off the ladder. Another warrior armed with a spear soon took his place at the top of the ladder, and Corvo swayed just in time to avoid a powerful thrust. Using the reach advantage his spear gave him, the grinning warrior was able to keep Corvo at a distance while he climbed onto the rampart. Thrust after thrust was made in Corvo's direction, but he managed to avoid them all. Behind the warrior, two others, one armed with a ferocious-looking war axe and the other a spear, had also managed to scramble onto the ramparts and more were coming.

Corvo could not tell what was happening anywhere else in the fort; his fight and his life were a handful of paces in front of him.

Two warriors rushed past him but didn't attack, their sights set on other Romans farther along the ramparts. The warrior with the spear lunged again, and Corvo avoided it by swaying left. Then he thrust towards Corvo's face and Corvo only just managed to get his gladius in the way in time to deflect the point. The warrior was clearly tiring of the duel; if Corvo could show patience, the man would make a mistake and he could end this.

The warrior made two more thrusts at Corvo, the first one striking his shoulder armour and the second again being deflected by his gladius. This time, while the spear point was beyond him, Corvo raced in low and shoulder-barged the warrior, sending him stumbling backwards. Corvo followed him and before the man could recover, thrust his gladius into his groin. The warrior howled with pain, dropped his spear and fell to his knees. The man would be dead in a matter of moments, and more and more warriors were making it onto the ramparts, so Corvo moved on.

A young warrior with a two-handed axe took a huge swing at Corvo, but it was easy for Corvo to predict its trajectory. He ducked below it and then drove his gladius into the man's belly, twisting the blade before withdrawing it. Another warrior appeared in front of him, a young man probably taking part in his first battle. His spear thrusts were tentative and lacked confidence, and Corvo was soon able to deflect the shaft long enough for him to get inside its reach and stab the man in the chest.

When that warrior dropped to the ground, Corvo registered a flicker of movement in front of him and ducked just in time as a small axe was hurled in his direction. It struck something behind him, but he had no time to see what as the axe-thrower was already reaching for another weapon. Corvo bent and picked up a fallen warrior's spear. Its design and quality was much cruder than the Roman pilum, but from that distance Corvo didn't think he could miss. He threw it without hesitation, striking the warrior in the middle of the chest and sending him stumbling backwards over the rampart edge.

For a few precious moments, the rampart immediately in front of him was clear, though numerous melees and duels were taking place elsewhere along the northern rampart. Corvo glanced to his right and saw that Tribune Crispus and the men under his command were just about holding the eastern rampart. To his left, Tribune Ortius and his men were greatly reduced in numbers and were being driven back. Without help they would not be able to hold. Down in the square, Titus Galba's experienced eye had seen the danger and was rushing the men under his command to the tribune's aid. He clearly planned on trapping the tribesmen on that rampart between the two forces and crushing them.

"Marcus!" The shout was urgent and laced with panic and although Corvo did not recognise the voice, the warning it offered was clear. He had lingered too long and allowed himself to become distracted by everything going on around him. Now a cluster of warriors, maybe six or seven, were racing towards him. He didn't stand a chance, yet he had nowhere to run. Looking around, he quickly found what he was looking for and picked up a fallen shield, preparing to meet the warriors' charge. They were no more than twenty paces from him when somebody behind him shouted.

"Corvo, drop!"

Corvo didn't hesitate. Thinking a bowman had seen the danger and was going to try and take down at least one of the warriors for him, he had instantly dropped to his knees. Crouching behind his shield, he stared over its iron rim at the men charging towards him. But it hadn't been a bowman who had called his name. Instead, he watched as one of the big scorpio bolts slammed into the lead warrior, its tip travelling clean through the man's body and into the warrior behind him as well, killing them both instantly. The impact had been so powerful that both men had been knocked off their feet and hurled backwards into their comrades. Two of these were sent plummeting off the ramparts to their deaths, while another was sent crashing to the rampart floor.

Corvo was on his feet in a flash and had raced over and stabbed the fallen man in the chest before he could regain his feet. The remaining two warriors had just about recovered from the shock of seeing so many of their comrades killed in one fell swoop and now launched themselves at Corvo, seeking revenge. Corvo used his shield to block one man's downward slice and flicked out with his own gladius at the other, leaving the warrior with a deep gash across the front of his right thigh. The first warrior swung at Corvo again and Corvo once more blocked his attack with his shield before putting his weight behind it and shoving the man backwards. His own momentum had carried him further than he'd anticipated, though, and in doing so he had left his right side open for the second warrior to attack, which he made to do. Corvo tried to turn but knew he would be too late. To his surprise, the warrior's look of triumph turned into a grimace of shock and pain as an arrow went through one cheek and out the other. He silently fell backwards into the square.

The remaining warrior had by now recovered his feet and launched himself at Corvo with a flurry of blows, each of which was met by the Roman's shield. It was taking its toll, though, and his arm had begun to ache from constantly lifting the heavy shield and the juddering each stroke caused. Realising he had to try something different, Corvo held his shield high, looked down at the rampart in front of him and took a pace backwards. When the warrior stepped forward, following him, and his foot came into sight, Corvo slammed the iron rim of his shield down onto the man's toes as hard as he could, before quickly raising it again. He was rewarded with the sound of crunching bones. The warrior screamed and stopped swinging his sword. Seizing his moment, Corvo lowered his shield and thrust his gladius over the top, into the bottom of the man's throat. For a few moments nothing happened, and then the man's sword fell from his grasp and there was a heavy thud as he dropped to the rampart floor.

Corvo took a moment to look around him just as the tribesmen's horns rang out, ordering a retreat just like they had earlier in the day. The north rampart on which he stood was virtually clear of warriors, those that remained either trying to make it back to the ladders or still engaged in one-to-one fights with legionaries. The western rampart which at one stage had looked as if it were about to be overrun, was now completely clear of enemy combatants, Titus Galba's timely intervention with his reserves having saved the day. The eastern rampart was still alive with numerous fights, but already legionaries from other points around the fort were racing towards it, and the odds would soon swing inexorably in the defenders' favour. The tribesmen had to choose whether to try and escape back over the wall or die fighting. There was no way they could prevail now.

Corvo slowly made his way towards the far western end of the northern rampart, pausing twice to finish off wounded tribesmen. At the far end of the rampart, Centurion Jovian was helping the crew of one of the scorpiones to turn the weapon so that it was once again pointing out across the clearing and towards the forest.

"My thanks, Jovian. You and your men saved my life."

"You're welcome. A bloody day."

"Very," replied Corvo, glancing about him at the carpet of dead bodies. There were far too many dead Romans for his liking. "Still, at least we held."

Jovian nodded. "For now, but I'd wager we won't be able to withstand another assault like that. All right, men, that will do. Festus, take Alba down to see the surgeon and get that wound seen to, then go and find yourselves something to eat and drink."

"What about you, sir?" Festus asked.

"I'll see to myself when you get back. Besides, Alba's bleeding all over my clean rampart and it's starting to annoy me. Now go before I change my mind."

Corvo laughed as he watched the two legionaries hurry away. "Careful, Jovian, you're in danger of becoming a good man."

"No, I don't think so. I just like to show a softer side every now and again. It confuses them and keeps them on their toes," replied Jovian, grinning.

"Do you need help with anything?"

"No, we've got the scorpio back in position, though with only two bolts left it's about as much use as a eunuch in a brothel."

"Well then, let's hope the chieftain decides that it's costing him too many of his warriors to keep attacking the fort and they crawl off back to their forest."

"I think we both know that's not very likely, Corvo. I leave fantasies like that to men like Tribune Ortius."

Corvo laughed. "Yes, I've no doubt you're right. Anyway, my thanks again." He turned to return along the rampart towards the gates and the steps down to the square. Behind him, Centurion Jovian had begun whistling a tune that Corvo found oddly familiar. He joined in when he finally recognised it, but almost as soon as he did so, Jovian stopped. Curious as to why, Corvo turned to speak to the centurion, the smile on his face evaporating at the sight before him. The older centurion sat with his back to the scorpio, clutching his left side, blood seeping through his fingers.

Corvo raced along the rampart to Jovian's side, trying to assess the severity of the wound, but he couldn't persuade Jovian to move his hand away from it.

"What happened?"

"One of them wasn't as dead as he was making himself out to be. I turned my back and the next thing I knew, some bastard had stabbed me in the side."

"How bad is it?"

"Bad enough. He went over the wall."

Corvo hurried to the palisade just in time to see a warrior climb off the ladder. Perhaps sensing he was being watched, the warrior glanced up at the rampart. His eyes met Corvo's, and he grinned, the grin of a man who knew he had just stared death in the face and escaped. When Corvo stepped out of sight and reappeared a few moments later brandishing a spear, the warrior's grin disappeared, and he turned to run.

Hefting the spear in his hand, Corvo drew his right arm back and threw the spear as hard as he could at the tribesman's back. Its point harmlessly sunk into the soft ground a couple of strides in front of the warrior, bringing him to a sudden halt. He again turned and grinned at Corvo. Then, almost as an afterthought, he dropped his breeches and bent over, exposing his backside in his direction.

"Did you get the bastard?" asked a weak voice from behind Corvo.

Corvo turned to look at Jovian, who was turning a deathly grey. He considered lying to him to give him some peace of mind in what may well be his last moments, but he decided the man deserved better.

"No, sorry, Jovian. Not the best with spears, especially barbarian ones," he said apologetically.

"A pity, but no matter. Could never master the damn things myself."

A cry from outside the fort walls drew Corvo's attention and he glanced out to find the Germani warrior now struggling to pull his breeches up, his task made considerably more difficult by the arrow protruding from his right buttock. Corvo glanced to his right and saw the Syrian archer Kochar waving at him. Corvo waved his thanks just as Flavius and Atilus made their way along the rampart towards Corvo and Jovian.

Jovian watched Corvo walk a few paces and then pick up another tribesman's spear before walking back to his original position.

"You fancy another shot?" asked Jovian. "What makes you think you'll have better luck this time, when he's farther away? You'll just be wasting another spear we could use when the tribesmen come back."

"Our friend is somewhat hindered now," said Corvo. While he had been searching for another spear, Kochar had struck the warrior with another arrow, this one piercing his left heel.

"How so?" asked Jovian, before coughing up some blood and spitting it onto the rampart.

"Kochar, the Syrian archer has slowed him down with two arrows, one in the heel and one in his buttocks. He's trying to crawl away with his breeches around his ankles. He had been showing us his rear end before the arrows hit."

By now Flavius and Atilus had reached the two men.

"Jovian, you're hurt!" exclaimed Flavius. "Let me get you to the surgeon."

"Not yet. Centurion Corvo here is going to try and skewer the bastard who did this for me."

The two men walked to the palisade to stand next to Corvo and look out over the clearing.

"The man whose rear end is in the air, looking like a porcupine?" asked Atilus.

"Yes, him."

"The arrows are Kochar's work?"

"They are," replied Corvo, drawing his arm back to throw again before the tribesman managed to crawl out of range.

"You'll never hit him like that," said Atilus.

"You may be better than me, Atilus, but I think even I can hit a man crawling along the ground at that pace."

"Really? If you say so," replied Atilus, stepping back.

Corvo could tell by his tone that he very much doubted it. He sighed. "Oh, very well, you take the throw. I will never hear the end of it if I miss." He passed the spear to Atilus without looking at his face.

"I don't care who, but can one of you just take the damn throw before I die down here waiting? I want to walk through the gates of Elysium knowing that the man who killed me went first," snapped Jovian.

Corvo, Atilus and Flavius all nodded at him before turning back to look out at the tribesman. The spear was in the air before Corvo realised it. As if sensing its approach, the tribesman had stopped crawling and half turned to look back towards the fort. Moments later, the spear struck him square in the middle of the back and he collapsed into the dirt.

Flavius let out a long, low whistle of admiration. "No, Atilus was right, you'd never have made that shot, Marcus."

"Thanks for the show of confidence, Optio Flavius." He glared at Atilus, who was grinning from ear to ear. Then, breaking into a smile himself, Corvo slapped the former gladiator on the shoulder. "Well done, my friend."

"He's dead?" asked Jovian from where he leant against the scorpio.

"Very," replied Flavius.

"Then all of you can clear off and leave me to die in peace, if you don't mind."

"Enough of the drama, Centurion Jovian. It's only a scratch; you'll be fine soon enough," said Corvo.

Everyone there knew that was a lie, Jovian most of all, but they all played along with the charade.

"Then at least get me somewhere warm; my manhood has nearly shrivelled up, it's so cold." The blood loss was clearly taking its toll.

Corvo saw Legionary Felix walk past in the square below, Legionary Fabianus at his side as always. "Felix, Fabianus, up here on the double." Both men looked up and came running when they saw Centurion Corvo's stern demeanour. "Get the centurion to the surgeon as fast as you can." The two legionaries lifted the wounded man as quickly as they could and carefully picked their way along the rampart and down the steps before crossing the square to the surgeon's hall.

"Do you think he's going to make it?" asked Flavius.

"No," replied Atilus. "I have seen many men with similar wounds die in the arena. His passing may be long, but he will pass."

"He's a tough old boot. He might make it yet," added Corvo, but he knew that Atilus almost certainly spoke the truth.

CHAPTER 13

The tribesmen did not attack again that day and by early evening, Legate Crispus felt comfortable enough to call an officers' briefing, leaving double the number of sentries he would do normally on guard. Corvo was surprised to see a familiar face in the legate's room when he arrived for the briefing.

"Legionary Gemmellus, I thought you'd got lost," said Corvo, smiling and offering the other man his arm.

Gemmellus laughed, taking the joke as it was meant, as Corvo knew that Gemmellus was the best scout and tracker in the three forts.

"It is good to see you too, Centurion Corvo," he replied, clasping the centurion's arm. "I thought I'd come back rather than let you have all the fun."

"Where have you been? We were expecting you back sooner."

"I went to…"

"Men, if it's all right with you, I would like to chair my meeting?" said Legate Crispus, interrupting them.

"Sorry, Legate, of course," replied Corvo.

"Thank you. Well, as you can see, Legionary Gemmellus has returned to us. As you may recall I sent him to escort Cornelius Arus to Fort Voltera, where Arus was to try and impress upon Tribune Helvius the urgent need for him to cross the Rhenus in support of us, something he has hitherto been reluctant to do. As I have said before, I suspected that it was because he had been ordered not to do so either by Legate Scipio or the emperor, rather than because of a lack of

161

courage. A matter of conjecture — until now. Arus sends word via Gemmellus here that the tribune wishes to march to our aid but has been ordered by Legate Scipio not to do so without his direct permission. He does not seem minded to disobey that order, though Arus is convinced the man is genuine in his desire to help us. The men under his command are also unhappy, Arus tells me, and wish to march to their brothers' aid. It is causing some friction between the Twenty-Second and the Twentieth, apparently."

"But why will Legate Scipio not let them come to the aid of their fellow countrymen?" asked Tribune Ortius.

"As I have said before, at least to some of you, the emperor sees my previous successes as a threat, possibly even to his throne, though Mithras knows nothing could be further from my mind. He has sent me here to be disgraced or better still, killed. By withholding those men and refusing to let me retreat over the bridge, he is in all likelihood expediting the matter. And then there's the fact that Legate Scipio is a very ambitious man and has rarely, if ever, seen eye to eye with me. Which means that for the time being at least, we are on our own and on the wrong side of the Rhenus with some very angry tribesmen keen to part our heads from our necks. We have but one thing to decide: do we stay and fight, or do we defy orders and make a break for it? Thoughts? And please speak freely; for now, at least, there is no rank inside these four walls."

"A moment ago, sir, you said the emperor is refusing to let you retreat over the bridge," said Corvo. "Surely you mean bridges? There are three within marching distance, are there not?"

"Very good, astute as always, Centurion Corvo. Legionary Gemmellus' return was delayed because the nearest bridge to Fort Felix was burned down and destroyed." An angry muttering swept through the cluster of officers. "We have reason to believe that only the Claudian bridge to the north-west remains."

"But that is several days' march away. How are you back so soon, Gemmellus?" asked Tribune Crispus. "You have not had time to march up there, cross and then travel back to Fort Felix."

"I had already crossed the next nearest bridge to Fort Felix when a band of tribesmen turned up. I hid and waited for them to depart before resuming my journey here," said Gemmellus.

"Then you don't know for sure that the bridge to the east is destroyed?" said Tribune Ortius. "You never saw that one put to the torch?"

"No I didn't, but the band of warriors arrived from the west, and it is a fair assumption that they had come from the other bridge and were planning on doing the same to that one."

"Then how do we know for certain that the Claudian bridge is still open? Surely it is likely that they started there and were working their way eastwards, destroying each bridge as they came across it?" said Corvo.

"We don't for certain, but I have a suspicion that they would not risk angering the Empire or the other local tribes by destroying every means of communication. Some of the other tribes would not take kindly to all their trade routes with the Empire being destroyed, and the chieftain isn't strong enough to fight us and other tribes at the same time. Besides, if we do decide to try and escape, we have to aim for somewhere, so we either head for the Claudian bridge or the bridge to the east, which we think has been destroyed," said the legate, his irritation beginning to show.

"Not a very satisfactory state of affairs," said Corvo.

"Quite. So what do we think — stay and fight with little hope of support, or flee and face the consequences?"

"They hit us hard this afternoon and our losses are extensive. We barely have enough men to man the ramparts now, let alone form any sort of effective strategic reserve," said Galba.

"They're learning, that's for sure," said the legate.

"I have a theory on that, Legate."

"You do? Then please share it, Centurion Corvo."

"When we attacked their camp, one of my men, a Germani by the name of Drax, absconded after killing two of my men. He told us that he once belonged to the Chatti tribe…"

"The Chatti? They live far to the north, do they not?" asked the legate.

"So I believe, Legate. I think, however, it would be prudent to assume that was a lie and that he once belonged to one of the local tribes hereabouts, perhaps even the one we are fighting. I think he has rejoined them and is now providing advice and guidance to their chieftain."

"And who is this Drax? Is he a former legionary or officer who knows our methods and tactics?"

"No, sir, he was a gladiator, and not one from the big arenas — more a brawler from the underground pits."

"Dear Mithras! How did you ever expect to control him? Those men are like rabid dogs."

"Although his attitude has been … challenging at times, he has largely obeyed orders and fought well … until now."

"What advice could a former pits gladiator possibly give to the chieftain about battle tactics? I think you're mistaken, Centurion."

"With respect, Legate, I don't think so. While he may not have served in the legions before, he was with us in Armenia and saw how we assaulted one town and defended a fort. He will have seen what I did and will have expected me to do the same again here. That is why they switched from an all-out catastrophic frontal assault, to a three-sided synchronised assault which very nearly led to them overwhelming us. It also explains their tactic of keeping those bowmen out of range of our ramparts — Drax told their chieftain that we would be running low on javelins and arrows and would try and recover some from outside the fort. If the chieftain had committed his reserves, they may have succeeded in overrunning us, and our heads would now be adorning stakes somewhere around his camp."

"A charming thought. So if we stay here and try and defend the fort, we are likely to be overrun because one of your former men has betrayed us, unless we try something different."

"Given our losses, Legate, I don't see us holding the fort whatever tactics we employ," said Centurion Galba, who had largely been silent to this point.

"Then you are for withdrawing?" asked the legate.

"I never like to run from a fight, Legate, but if we stay here it will become our tomb."

The legate nodded. "And the rest of you, do you agree with Centurion Galba?"

"With regret, yes, I do," answered Corvo.

Tribunes Ortius and Crispus nodded their agreement.

"What of Cornelius Arus, sir?" asked Corvo. "Is he returning?"

"Arus will be halfway to Rome by now, I suspect. Having tried and failed to persuade Tribune Helvius to march out with the men, he will no doubt be looking to secure us some sort of help in Rome, though what that may constitute I have no idea. The man is ever resourceful, however."

"I hate to be the one who casts doubt on all of this, but just how are we going to slip away from the fort unseen when they are watching us from the trees? Then there are the wounded. I just don't see how it can be done," said Tribune Crispus almost apologetically as he looked at his father.

"I have an idea on that too," said Corvo. "But it's not going to be popular," he added as he looked each man around the table in the eye.

"Another one! You're starting to put the rest of us to shame. Let's hear it then," said the legate.

A short while later, they all sat staring at Corvo, each man's expression different. Some were clearly supportive of his suggestion, others not so much.

"It's preposterous. You can't order them to do that," blustered Tribune Ortius.

"I wasn't planning on ordering anybody, sir, but the fact of the matter is the seriously wounded won't be able to carry out the first part of the plan, let alone the rest. These men know what the tribesmen will do to them if they take them alive, wounded or not. I am merely offering them the chance to gain a little bit of glory and die with honour," replied Corvo.

"Better they die fighting on their feet than in a bunk, Tribune," added Galba supportively.

"But what of those who cannot stand, the bedridden?"

"We will either despatch them ourselves or ask those that remain behind to do it for us when the time comes," said Corvo.

"Dear Mithras, you're a cold bastard, Corvo. These are dying men, our men," spat Ortius.

"Which is precisely why I don't want them to fall into the hands of the tribesmen. We have all seen what they do to their prisoners, Tribune. I know if I was one of the wounded I would either want to die fighting or have one of my friends give me a clean death before the enemy could get their hands on me." The two young men glared at one another, neither showing any inclination to back down.

"Do you have an alternative plan, Tribune?" asked the legate.

"Well, no, but…"

"But nothing. Time is against us and Corvo's is the only plan. Not only that, but I also think it has an outside chance of success," said the legate.

"If it works and we escape, what then, Legate?" asked his son. "You will likely be arrested and executed for disobeying the emperor's orders."

"Quite possibly. But you and some of the others will be safe, so it will not have been in vain."

"Not necessarily. The emperor is mad enough to visit a severe punishment on all of us."

"Well, it is a risk we will have to take if we are to follow Corvo's plan. There is no alternative, and each of you should come to terms with it."

"What of the silver?" All eyes turned to Galba. "We can't take it with us. Even if we were able to find a way to keep it from clinking, it will slow every man down."

"I have a plan for that too," said Corvo.

"I thought you might," said the legate with a smile.

"So all your efforts to retrieve the silver, all those lives lost, they are to be for nothing?" asked Tribune Crispus.

"It cannot be helped, Gaius," said his father.

"It is better than the alternative. I would rather live as a poor man than die as a rich one," said Corvo.

"Legate, I must protest against this course of action," said Tribune Ortius.

"Must you? I asked for honest opinions, and you have given me one, but the decision is made, now you must abide by it. This is the Roman army, not some weak Greek democracy. If you feel that strongly about it, Tribune, may I suggest that you remain behind with the wounded men? I'm sure seeing you ready to die at their side will stiffen their resolve. What do you think? No? I didn't think so. Now, enough, we're going to try Corvo's plan. Tonight is too soon, so we will attempt the escape tomorrow night. All we have to do in the meantime is survive tomorrow."

They had been attacked twice that day and were unlikely to survive another assault, so the chances of finding out whether Corvo's plan would work were slim at best anyway. Still, they had to try. After delegating duties for the coming day regarding the fort's defences, the briefing broke up. While Galba went to check the sentries and Corvo went away to think his plan through, the other officers headed for their bunks.

No attack came that night, nor the following morning, and none of the sentries reported even seeing a tribesman. Hope swept through the defenders that the Germani had had enough and withdrawn back into the forest to lick their wounds and mourn their dead, of which there were many. Corvo didn't believe it. Drax and the chieftain would be reviewing how their last attack went and coming up with a new plan, one that wouldn't be so costly in manpower. While he had no doubt the chieftain would be willing to expend all of his warriors to avenge the rape of his wife and the murder of his son, he doubted that his warriors would be quite so keen. Whatever he and Drax came up with this time would have to work.

The Germani archers emerged from the trees mid-afternoon and took up their earlier positions just outside bow range, their purpose once again to prevent the Romans from leaving the fort to retrieve javelins and arrows.

Corvo watched from his usual spot on the ramparts and was gratified to see that there were far fewer of them this time than before. They had tried to hide it by kneeling further apart so that the line was the same length, but there was no disguising the fact that their numbers had been considerably thinned.

Their chieftain obviously wasn't thinking clearly, otherwise he would have deployed his bowmen earlier; there had been nothing stopping the Romans venturing outside the fort that morning, and Corvo cursed himself silently for not having done exactly that. On reflection he realised that it would have made little difference, as those being left to guard the fort would mostly be unable to throw the javelins or pull a bowstring, and those leaving could only carry so much.

Corvo glanced back inside the fort, where at various positions around the grounds men were busy digging grave-size holes. He turned his gaze back towards the forest just as a handful of tribesmen emerged from the trees and stood behind their bowmen. It was difficult to see from that distance, but Corvo was quite sure that the chieftain was among them and if so, Drax probably was too. The tribesmen were staring at the fort, deep in discussion. Corvo just hoped that whatever they were planning, it wasn't going to happen that afternoon or worse still, that night. The longer he and his men had to try and put some distance between themselves and the fort, the better their chances of escape.

Corvo cast his mind back to earlier that morning, when he had visited the makeshift hospital to assess the wounded. Out of the sixty-seven currently receiving treatment, four were permanently bedridden and would be unable to take part in his proposed plan, and seven had superficial wounds that once bandaged would not stop them from carrying out normal duties. The remaining fifty-six had wounds that would prevent them from climbing ropes or carrying a heavy shield. It was these men that Corvo had mainly addressed.

Somehow, against all the odds, Centurion Jovian still drew breath, though nobody expected him to live much longer.

"To what do we owe the pleasure of your company in this house of the dead and dying?" Jovian had said earlier that morning, when he had spotted Corvo watching him from the doorway.

"You're still with us, Jovian? Are you such a bad soldier that you can't even die when you're supposed to?" replied Corvo, striding over to where Jovian lay propped up.

"I am, despite the best efforts of the surgeons. I keep telling them to leave me alone and let me die in peace, but they don't listen. Butchers, the lot of them." Jovian stopped and stared at Corvo. "What ails you, Corvo? You look exhausted."

Corvo gave a weak smile. "That obvious, eh?"

"You've got a face like a man who's been wandering through the desert for days without a drink and who finally arrives at a well to find it's got a dead goat in it. Tell me the problem — what's it going to do, kill me?" Jovian laughed.

"That's not too far from the truth actually."

"Now I have to know." Jovian's eyes darted around the room until they settled on a young orderly, who was rushing about. "You! Fetch the centurion here a stool and be quick about it, or I might soil my bed again just for you." The orderly swallowed hard and then hurried off, arriving back a few moments later carrying a small wooden stool, which he dutifully placed at the head of Jovian's bed.

"Poor boy is terrified of you," said Corvo, sitting down as the orderly rushed off.

"So he should be, rampart-dodger."

"Don't be too hard on him … any of them. We've all got our job to do."

Jovian narrowed his eyes. "Something tells me that's what you're here to see me about."

Corvo nodded and leaned forward. "They hit us hard last time, Jovian."

"I know. I was there," replied Jovian, pointing to his wound.

"Yes, sorry, I meant…"

"Oh, for the love of Mithras! Spit it out, Corvo, before you bore me to death."

"We have no chance."

"Now I understand you. Why didn't you say that in the first place?" Jovian shook his head. "So what plan have you and the legate concocted this time?"

"This one is all on me."

"Very well — what plan have you concocted?"

Corvo proceeded to tell Jovian everything that had been discussed at the previous night's officers' meeting. Jovian was silent throughout and only nodded when it was apparent Corvo had finished.

"So what do you think?"

"I think your description of our position was accurate."

"And the part these men will need to play?" asked Corvo, waving an arm around the room.

"They're good men, Centurion. They'll do what you ask, and so will I. Wasn't planning on dying in this bed anyway."

"And the men who can't get out of their beds?"

Jovian knew what Corvo was asking. "I'll see to it myself, if I'm able. If not, I'll make sure it's done properly and with dignity."

Corvo nodded solemnly. "Jovian, I'm sorry. If there was any other way, I'd…"

"I'm not asking for your pity. I've had a good run, and truth be told I should have died up on that rampart yesterday. By the grace of Mithras I didn't, so I was spared for a reason, and that reason is to help these men buy you and the others enough time to escape. If I can do that, I'll die a happy man, if not a rich one. Speaking of which, what about the coins belonging to these men? You can't leave them here, otherwise all those men died for nothing in the forest."

"Most of it is being left behind. We can't afford to be weighed down or risk making any noise. We'll have a few coins each at best."

"For my part, I'd be grateful if you took at least some of my share and used it to pay for drinks in my memory when you get back to safety."

"No wife or children?" asked Corvo, surprised.

"You know as well as I do that men below the rank of centurion aren't officially allowed to take a wife — that's why the whorehouses do so well out of us."

"But you're a centurion."

"Yes, but since becoming one all those years ago I've never met anyone I wanted to be shackled to. As for children, every man under my command behaves like a child, so I've had my fill of them. No, you take my silver if you're able and you make sure that whatever men survive this hole have a good drink on me."

"You can count on it."

"I know I can. Now, I think you'd better tell these men the plan so we can start getting ready if you're off tonight."

Corvo nodded and after much cajoling finally managed to get the attention of all but the very grievously wounded in the hospital. The news of their situation and his plan was received with muted acceptance. Those badly wounded knew that whether the troops stayed or fled, they would in all likelihood die, and most relished the chance to spit in the eye of death one last time. Some of those with arm or leg wounds said that they would leave with the able-bodied men, but when Corvo patiently explained that their escape depended on being able to scale walls and descend ropes with speed and in silence, they reluctantly accepted their fate. The chief surgeon blustered and railed at Corvo for deserting his men, and Corvo sat silently while he unloaded his anger. Finally, realising the hopelessness of the situation, the surgeon calmed down, and Corvo instructed him to make preparations to leave. The surgeon laughed and stated that his place was with the wounded and that he would not desert them. The junior surgeon and the orderlies, although somewhat more reluctantly, also said that they would remain behind to tend to the wounded.

Corvo's mind was dragged back to the present when Tribune Crispus asked him a question.

"Are they getting ready for another attack, do you think, Centurion?"

"I think so, but not today," Corvo replied. He watched as the chieftain and the group of men with him turned and melted back into the forest.

"What were you thinking about before I disturbed you?"

"The wounded, and whether I'm doing the right thing in leaving them here to die."

"You're leaving them here to die with honour — there is a difference. If we all stay and fight, there's every chance we will all be slaughtered. Their noble sacrifice will give the rest of us a fighting chance."

"A slim one at best."

"Yet a chance nonetheless."

"They won't be able to hold them very long, Tribune."

"I know, but every moment they do delay them is a moment we can put more ground between them and us."

"The journey to the Claudian bridge is long, through forests the tribesmen know well. And even if we do somehow stay ahead of them, we might arrive to find the bridge destroyed."

"Or we might find the legions camped there, on their way to meet us."

"I think we both know that is most unlikely."

"One problem at a time, eh, Marcus? It is a good plan, and we will all do our best to make it succeed. If the gods do not favour us, then there is not much we can do about it except seek a glorious death."

"I can tell you've been spending too much time in Lucius' company. His perennial positive outlook is rubbing off on you."

Tribune Crispus laughed and slapped Corvo on the shoulder. "Right, I'd better go and kick a few backsides. I'm officer of the watch for the next few hours."

"Yes, and I'd better go and check how preparations for tonight are going." Corvo made his way towards the steps leading down to the square below.

CHAPTER 14

No attack came that afternoon and as dusk fell, the chieftain even withdrew his bowmen, seemingly confident that the Romans would not venture outside the safety of their walls in the dark for fear of being rushed.

Corvo breathed a deep sigh of relief. Now he just had to pray that the tribesmen wouldn't have been persuaded by Drax to try a night-time assault. He suspected that most if not all of the warriors would prefer the comfort and safety of their campfires and the chance to drink.

As soon as it had grown dark, the preparations within the fort began to gather pace. First, the unpleasant task of carrying the bodies of their dead comrades up to the ramparts was carried out. The dead from the first assault had been burned, but the dead from the second attack, of which there were many, still lay untouched. Those who from a distance did not look as if they had any wounds were propped upright, leaning against the palisade. Corvo hoped to make the fort look fully manned so that it would give the attacking tribesmen something else to think about. Once they started to climb and breach the ramparts, the ruse would be up, but by then Corvo hoped that he and his men would be long gone.

The fifty-six wounded men had donned what armour and uniform they could so that from a distance they would look like functioning soldiers. They would be dotted along the fort's west, east and north walls and would walk up and down as much as they could to make the ramparts look a hive of activity and fully garrisoned. When they were no longer able to march up and down, they could rest on the stools that had been placed along the ramparts.

Those who could demonstrate that they were still capable of effectively throwing a javelin were issued with one, though few were now available and none of the men who were to remain were archers. Other than that, each man carried a gladius and a pugio. Each of the two bolt-throwing scorpiones only had two bolts remaining.

So that the men did not need to risk further injury by climbing up and down the steps, buckets of water were left along the ramparts, with empty buckets for them to urinate in. These men would live out their final hours up there.

At the rear of the fort, out of sight of any prying Germani eyes, ladders captured from the tribesmen were stacked against the walls ready to be slid over the palisade, and ropes had been secured ready to be thrown to the ground. The men who were to leave the fort had started to quietly gather there and were checking their kit to make sure nothing clinked or rattled. If the action they were about to undertake hadn't been so dangerous, Corvo would have laughed at the comical sight of scores of legionaries jumping up and down, listening for tell-tale noises which could be the difference between life and death.

Tearing his gaze away from them, he decided to pay one more visit to the makeshift hospital, now home to only four patients. The senior surgeon glared at him as he entered and then went back to whatever he was doing. Corvo glanced around and saw the gladius lying on the surgeon's desk. The junior surgeon had a gladius strapped to his waist.

"Are you sure you won't reconsider and come with us, Polonius?"

The Greek surgeon looked up and sadly shook his head. "No, my place is here. I will do what I can for these men until… Then I will man the ramparts with the others. But my staff should go, especially the boys." He nodded towards the two frightened-looking orderlies, one of whom was looking at the gladius he had been given as if it were a foreign object. "They insist they won't leave me."

"We can force them, if you like?" offered Corvo.

"No. It is for every man to choose his destiny, and they have chosen theirs, even if it is misguided."

"If the rest of the men staying here show half as much courage and diligence as you and your staff, then the Germani are going to have a difficult fight on their hands. I salute you … all of you." Corvo looked each of the four staff in the eye and then with a last look at the four men lying in their bunks, seemingly oblivious to their fate, he saluted and then turned to leave for the last time.

"Centurion Corvo," the chief surgeon called after him.

"Surgeon?"

"Make this all worth it. Get the men to safety."

Corvo nodded but didn't answer, the lump in his throat preventing words. Then he turned and left.

"Ah, there you are, Centurion Corvo. I was wondering where you'd got to," said Legate Crispus as Corvo emerged from the hospital into the fort's square.

"Just checking that everything was ready in the hospital, sir."

"And is it?"

"Yes, just four men remaining, plus the four staff. I have offered them the chance to come with us, but Surgeon Polonius is adamant that his place is here, and his staff won't leave him."

"It is their choice, Centurion Corvo."

"I know, and with that in mind, sir, I would respectfully request that I be allowed to remain behind and oversee the fort's defence."

The legate looked at Corvo as if he'd gone mad. "You're serious, aren't you?"

"I am. It only seems right, sir."

"Well, my answer is no. It's your plan and you need to be with us to see it through. Request denied."

"But…"

"No buts, Centurion, and that's an end to it." Someone caught the legate's eye. "Centurion Jovian! You're not dead!"

The old centurion made his way slowly over to where the two men stood and gave a salute as best he could. "No, sir, I'm not, but if you care to come back in a few hours, I think those men in the trees will have remedied that for me."

Both the legate and Corvo smiled. "Centurion Corvo here has asked to stay and command the defence of the fort, and I have told him no. What do you think, Centurion Jovian?"

The old centurion fixed his gaze on the younger centurion. "I think Centurion Corvo should leave these things to the grown-ups, sir. It took me about an hour to get dressed so I could lead the defence of this place, and I wouldn't take kindly to being usurped after all that."

"There you are, Centurion Corvo. You're not needed. Now, it will soon be time to leave, and I expect you have some final checks to carry out."

"Yes, sir." Corvo turned to face Jovian. "Courage and honour, Centurion Jovian."

"Courage and honour, Corvo. Now, if you'll both excuse me, if I start to make my way up to scorpio number one, I should just about get there before the tribesmen arrive in a few hours."

Corvo nodded and Jovian turned and slowly began to make his way across the square to the steps leading to the north rampart.

"How long do you think they'll last, Corvo?" asked the legate.

"Once the tribesmen are on the ramparts and discover the ruse? Not long, but with men like him standing their ground, how can we fail?" Corvo then turned and headed to where his men were mustering, ready to leave.

"Everything ready, Centurion Galba?"

Galba turned as Corvo approached. "I believe so."

"And what of the coins?"

"Every man is carrying his and a bit extra. What we couldn't carry has either been buried where the tribesmen won't find it, especially if they burn this place down, or scattered around the place like you ordered. We just have to keep an eye on the men to make sure they don't go picking it up on the sly."

"Maybe we'll be able to come back and retrieve it at some point in the future."

"Maybe," replied Galba, but neither man believed it. "Do you think they'll fall for it?"

Corvo stroked his chin as he considered it. "Maybe, maybe not, but either way it was worth a try."

After initially agreeing that the men were only to take a few coins with them, the officers had changed their minds when the demeanour of the legionaries had soured at the news that they were to leave their newfound wealth behind for the tribesmen. So long as they were able to secure it silently about their person, they could now bring what they wanted. It was, however, made clear to everyone that anybody who fell behind because of that burden would be left to their own devices. There would be no exceptions. The silver they couldn't carry was hidden beneath the legate's briefing room and some coins were scattered over the ground to make it look as if the money had been hurriedly buried. Those who did not know Corvo's plan thought that the holes he had the men digging were graves, but in actual fact they were immediately filled in. Some had a handful of coins tossed in before being refilled, others didn't. Corvo hoped that once the tribesmen overran the fort, they would think the holes contained the silver and would waste time excavating them while his men made good their escape.

Corvo looked up at the dark sky with its myriad pricks of light. He judged it to be fast approaching prima noctis hora. "It's time. Get the ladders and ropes over the wall," he said decisively.

Galba strode off and started quietly giving instructions. Ropes were dropped over the southern wall, while the ladders they had stolen from the tribesmen were carefully lowered over the side and then propped up. In the dark it was difficult to see if these had come to rest on even and firm ground, and it would take courage to climb over the palisade and onto a precarious ladder. With that in mind, Corvo decided that when his turn came, he would climb down using the rope.

Most of the torches save for the ones on the north rampart had been extinguished to try and disguise their departure from any eagle-eyed lookouts, so climbing over the palisade was difficult and perilous. But slowly and for the most part silently, the men began to disappear. Twice two of the ladders wobbled violently and nearly toppled, but quick-thinking men had grabbed the top and strained every sinew to hold them in place. Corvo watched and decided that his decision to use the rope to climb down was a good one. He had also persuaded the legate to use the rope. Both Galba and Felix had opted for the rope too, but in their case it was for fear of the ladders being unable to bear their weight.

When the last man was safely down, Corvo looked up and signalled to the two men left on the ramparts, and they began hauling the ladders up and pulling the ropes in. Corvo was grateful that he couldn't make out their faces in the dark. With one last wave, he pushed his way through his men to the front, where the legate was waiting with Gemmellus and Vortrix.

"Now is your time. Get us safely to the Claudian bridge," said Corvo.

Without saying a word, Vortrix hurried off to scout the way ahead while Gemmellus led the column, Corvo and the others falling silently into step behind them.

Galba and Flavius were to bring up the rear to make sure they weren't being followed and that nobody fell out of step or wandered off. A single mistake could give them all away, and Corvo was determined that wasn't going to happen.

There was a full moon, and the sky was almost cloudless. That meant they could see their way more clearly, but it also put them at greater risk of being discovered. They were all going to have to be vigilant.

As the eastern horizon started to lighten, heralding the start of another day, Vortrix returned, spoke to Gemmellus and suddenly turned north. When Corvo caught up with them and queried the change in direction, the scouts explained that now that daylight was approaching, they could no longer walk alongside the river and needed to head deep into the forest to mask their presence.

"Very well. Take us as far as you feel necessary, and then we will stop and have a short rest. The journey will be tougher and no doubt slower in the forest, but we must push on," said Corvo.

The two scouts nodded and then continued forward. After a while, Gemmellus gave the signal to stop as they entered a small clearing, an oasis of green in the dark forest. Corvo gave the order to fall out and rest for a short while, then detailed men to keep watch. As he sat, once again he thought morosely of the men they had left behind.

CHAPTER 15

Back at Fort Felix, Centurion Jovian winced as he twisted to speak to one of his men. The pain was becoming almost unbearable, but he prayed to Mithras for strength so that he could stand and lead his men in this final battle. The fact that he was still alive was a miracle, and he could only assume that the gods had deigned to let him live so that he could perform this one last duty. He would not let them down, and neither would his men.

"Put your back into it, Seponius! You're not dead yet!" he barked at the legionary struggling to load and crank the scorpio behind him. Jovian gritted his teeth and helped the other man to perform his task, panting from the exertion.

"It's a good job we've only got two bolts, Centurion. Any more and the effort would kill us, never mind the barbarians," said Seponius.

"I think you're right. Let's make sure the effort was worth it, eh? Only fire this thing at clusters of the tribesmen so we can take as many of them with us as we can!"

The young legionary was bearing a nasty leg wound that made moving difficult and painful. He wouldn't have been able to climb out of the fort, much less march at pace through difficult terrain. Jovian felt sorry for him; Seponius had only been with the legions for a few months and had had his whole life ahead of him. Now it was all about to be taken away. Jovian, however, had served the legions for more than twenty years and had seen much of the known world. It was perhaps, his time.

"Centurion, do you think the men who left will survive?" asked Seponius, breaking into Jovian's thoughts.

Jovian looked northwest, the direction in which Corvo and his men would be heading. "I don't know, son, but I have a feeling that if anyone can get them to safety, it's Centurion Corvo." He noticed that the young legionary was staring wistfully in the same direction. "Don't be envious of them, Legionary Seponius. All the fun is going to happen right here. You wouldn't want to miss out on that, would you?" Jovian was smiling broadly, and Seponius couldn't help responding in kind, though both wished that they were elsewhere.

"No, Centurion."

"Right, the scorpio is loaded and the men are as prepared as I can make them. There's no sign of the tribesmen, so I'm going to go down to the hospital and speak to the surgeon."

A look of terror spread across Seponius' face. "You're coming back, though, aren't you, Centurion? Before they get here, I mean?"

At any other time, Jovian would have berated the young soldier for cowardice and weakness, but not now. He understood. They were spread thinly on the ramparts, often with nobody but the dead for company, and Seponius wanted to know that somebody would be there to fight and die alongside him.

Jovian smiled. "I'll be back, son, don't you worry. I've something I've got to take care of down in the hospital, then I'll be right back. If they show their ugly faces before I return, you shout or send a runner to fetch me immediately, understood?"

Seponius nodded. "But, Centurion…"

"What?"

"I don't think there's anybody left in the fort capable of being a runner," Seponius said slowly, then broke into a smile when he realised that Jovian had been joking.

Jovian nodded and smiled. The young man was finding humour — that was good. It would help to combat the fear in the pit of his stomach. "Well, in that case find somebody who can limp fast."

Seponius laughed and the centurion joined in, the sound entirely incongruous to their situation. Many of the men stationed nearby turned to see what was so funny before resuming their solitary vigil.

Jovian slowly made his way along the rampart. Before descending the steps, he checked with the other scorpio crew that they were primed and ready.

"We've only got one bolt, though, Centurion, the other one is damaged," said one of the crew apologetically.

"Well, you'd better not miss then, had you?"

"We won't."

"I know you won't, men. Make it count," said Jovian, before gingerly descending the steps and making his way across the square towards the hospital. He paused before opening the door and stepping inside. With only four patients now within its walls and an equal number of staff, the place was eerily quiet compared to normal. Each patient had either a surgeon or orderly sitting next to them.

The chief surgeon got to his feet when he saw the centurion walk in and quietly made his way over to him.

"Centurion Jovian, are you all right? Do you need me to tend to your wound?"

"No, I'm fine. Well, you know — I'm still alive … for now."

"Then what are you doing here? I would have thought your place was out on the walls, commanding the men."

"It is, but as you know, Surgeon, I promised Centurion Corvo that I would not let any of the men fall into the hands of those bloody barbarians. I'm here to … well, you know what I'm here to do." To emphasise his point, Jovian moved his hand to the hilt of his gladius. "They won't feel a thing, I promise you. They all look asleep anyway," he added, glancing around the room.

"Well, you needn't concern yourself, Centurion. I have done your work for you."

"I don't understand."

"Each man has been given a concoction of medication and has slipped into a deep unconsciousness from which they will not wake." As he spoke, the surgeon watched as one of the orderlies lifted the wrist of the man he was watching over and felt for a pulse. Evidently not finding one, the orderly slowly stood and drew the bedsheet up and over the man's head. He glanced at the surgeon and then nodded. "There, we have lost two already. Mine passed just before you entered the room, and the others won't be far behind."

"You shouldn't have done that — it is against your beliefs. I was prepared to spare you that horror," said Jovian.

"I know," said the surgeon, patting Jovian on his shoulder, "and I am grateful, but you have enough worries, and I have tended these men. It was only right that I sent them peacefully on their way to Elysium." As he spoke, he watched the junior surgeon pull the sheet over his charge's head, having also just checked for a pulse. The surgeon walked over to where the last patient alive lay, with an orderly rigidly staring at him. The surgeon gently ushered the man out of the way and lifted the patient's wrist. After a few moments he placed a couple of fingers on the man's neck, trying to find a pulse. Having not done so, he covered the man's face with the bedsheet. "He's gone, son," he said kindly to the young orderly. "There, it is done," he added, turning to face Centurion Jovian.

Jovian nodded. "My thanks. Now, if you hurry, we can smuggle the four of you over the southern wall. If you hug the river northwest, you might pick up the trail of Corvo and the others. It's the best I can offer."

"That's kind of you, Centurion, but we've already discussed it and we'll stay, thank you."

"We are all going to die here. Me and the men, well, that's what we signed up for, but this isn't your fight. Go and try to save yourselves."

"Even if I wanted to, I'm too old to run, Centurion."

"But your staff…"

"Have chosen to remain and die with their comrades. Do not deny them that right."

"When did your hand last grasp a gladius, any of you?"

"We are all trained with weapons, Centurion. Don't you worry about us. We may not be your greatest warriors, but we won't die cheaply, will we, men?"

"No, sir," his staff replied in unison, though Jovian was sure at least one of the orderlies was shaking.

"Then it shall be an honour to have you alongside me."

"We shall try and treat the men as we go, to keep them in the fight for as long as possible, but once the rampart looks lost, we shall take our weapons and join the battle," said the chief surgeon.

"Thank you … all of you," said Jovian, a lump forming in his throat. "Just don't let yourselves be taken alive by those…"

"Fear not, Centurion, we probably know more ways to take our own lives than you could ever imagine. We will do what needs to be done if it becomes necessary."

Jovian nodded and was about to give them some advice when a barbarian horn reverberated through the air. The time to run had gone. The enemy were here.

Jovian glanced at the chief surgeon and then hurried out of the hospital and across the square. As he did so, he glanced up to where he had been standing a few moments before and saw Seponius looking anxiously in his direction. Jovian raised an arm to acknowledge the young soldier as he made his way to the steps. As he gingerly climbed up, he glanced about and was glad to see that the men were in position and looking out over the palisade towards the enemy.

When he reached the top of the steps, Jovian made his way to the palisade, nodding at the men nearby and trying to look confident. He hoped his face didn't betray his shock when his gaze fell on the scene before him. The chieftain had brought his entire force. He had also divided his warriors into three like last time and was obviously planning on hitting the north, west and east walls simultaneously again. Obviously confident that the Romans had few if any bowmen left, he had drawn his force up well within bow range, and his own archers were now shooting fire arrows into the fort's wooden gates.

It wasn't going to be a long battle, Jovian decided, but it should be a glorious one. Even if he'd thought it would make a difference, he realised that he didn't have any men to spare who could try to extinguish the flames that were now taking hold of the gates.

Arrows started to thump into the palisade now, others finding homes in shields or flesh. Jovian watched in despair as a legionary he didn't know the name of lowered his shield at the wrong moment. An arrow entered his mouth, piercing the back of his head, and the man fell silently backwards onto the ground below. Behind his fallen body, Jovian could see the chief surgeon and his three colleagues making their way to the northern ramparts. All were armed with a gladius, and one of the orderlies had also found a pilum. Jovian watched as the chief surgeon stopped briefly next to the man with an arrow through his mouth, then looked up and met his gaze. The chief surgeon said something to the three men with him and they all briefly embraced before making their way up the steps and spreading out. As the chief surgeon looked out over the palisade, an arrow whistled past his head and struck one of the orderlies in the chest, killing him instantly.

"I think we can dispense with the bandages we have brought with us. I don't think there will be time," said the chief surgeon, looking down at his fallen colleague. Though his expression was sorrowful, his tone was matter-of-fact.

"No, it doesn't look like it," replied Jovian, just as the warriors roared their battle cry and streamed towards the fort. "Good luck to you."

"You too, Centurion," said the chief surgeon, drawing his gladius.

To his right, Jovian heard the unmistakeable twang of a scorpio being fired. He looked out over the palisade just in time to see the bolt strike two warriors, pinning them together in a macabre embrace. Jovian nodded with satisfaction and turned to address the crew, but one of the two men had already been struck dead by a spear, and the other was hastily drawing his gladius as the first of the barbarians scaled the ladders below.

Jovian turned and hurried along the rampart to where he could see Seponius getting ready to fire the other scorpio. Jovian could feel that his wound had opened and was bleeding again, but it didn't matter. All that mattered in that moment was that he kept his word to the young legionary. He wouldn't let the young man die alone.

"Did you miss me, Legionary Seponius?" he asked when he came alongside the soldier. Seponius didn't reply but gave a terrified smile. "Let them have it, Legionary."

Seponius picked a target in the throng of warriors below and fired. The bolt took a big warrior's head clean off, spraying the men around him with a fountain of blood and causing them to stall in their advance. The horror of what they had just witnessed was enough to shrivel their courage, if only for a few moments.

A large warrior with a long, unkempt beard and wild eyes shoved and cajoled the men to keep moving, using his axe handle to strike one who looked like he was turning to flee. The man dropped to the ground, where moments later the large warrior removed his head with a powerful stroke of his war axe. He then glared at the men around him, and as one they turned and resumed their charge towards the fort. Clearly the thought of facing that warrior's wrath was more terrifying than any Roman weapon.

Jovian grunted — he had found the target for their last bolt. "Quickly, help me load!" he shouted at Seponius as he noticed that men were scaling the walls towards them. Seponius swung into action. By the time the scorpio was loaded, numerous ladders were against the wall and Jovian risked a glance over to see what was happening. That was a mistake, as an arrow fired by a warrior at the foot of the ladder struck Jovian in the left shoulder and he let out a scream of pain.

"Centurion!" Seponius shouted in alarm.

"I'm all right. I'm not dead yet, Seponius. Quick, help me turn this." Between them, they just about managed to turn the scorpio so that it was facing the palisade above where one of the ladders rested. Jovian took up position behind it and waited. Moments later a head appeared and as Jovian had hoped, it was the head of the large warrior who had killed his own man for cowardice. He glanced to his left as he clambered onto the rampart and then as he stood upright he glanced to his right to see the Roman bolt thrower pointing right at him. A grinning Jovian waved and then fired. From that distance the bolt hit him with such force that despite his size, it knocked him clean off his feet and back over the palisade to the ground below. He landed on several of his comrades, crushing them under his weight.

Jovian allowed himself a small laugh and turned to share it with Seponius. The young man's smile turned into a grimace of pain as a spear point emerged from his stomach. Seponius glanced down at the protruding iron then looked up at Jovian as the weapon was withdrawn. Blood escaped the corners of his mouth, and without a sound he collapsed to the ground to reveal a grinning warrior, who was one of several who had scaled the wall behind them. The look of rage on Jovian's face panicked the warrior and he hastily threw the spear, still wet with Seponius' blood, but Jovian just managed to duck behind his shield, which he had leaned against the scorpio. The warrior's spear crashed into the shield, and Jovian immediately discarded it. Then, drawing his gladius in one fluid movement, he raced as fast as he could towards the Germani warrior. Both of his wounds were now oozing blood, and the pain was terrible, but Jovian did his best to ignore it. All that mattered now was vengeance. The tribesman reached for his own sword, but being longer than the gladius, it was harder to draw. By the time it was clear of his belt, Jovian was already upon him. Jovian thrust his gladius deep into the warrior's chest before withdrawing his blade and pushing the man away.

Blood was flowing freely from Jovian's original wound now, and his shoulder hurt like Hades from the arrow that was still embedded in his flesh. He took a moment to glance round and assess the situation. All three ramparts had been breached and the ruse of placing dead men had been discovered, but only after the enemy had wasted arrows shooting them. Jovian silently congratulated Corvo on his cunning plan.

Looking around, Jovian knew that his men could not hold out for much longer; their number was already halved. On the eastern rampart he watched with fascination as the junior surgeon engaged in a swordfight with two warriors. The man was not without skill and as Jovian watched, he ran one of the warriors through. In doing so he had exposed his left flank, though, and before Jovian could shout a warning, the other warrior seized his opportunity and sliced into the surgeon's side. He dropped to the ground, and the tribesman began to hack him to pieces.

A roar from behind Jovian drew his attention and he cursed himself for becoming distracted, waiting for a blade to pierce his flesh at any moment, but none came. Instead he heard a grunt of pain and turned to see a large warrior, his weapon poised to strike, collapse backwards with a pilum in his chest. He fell heavily to the ground below. Jovian glanced behind him and saw the chief surgeon, covered in blood, nod at him.

Jovian nodded back and then turned to face a new challenge he could hear racing towards him. Two warriors were approaching, one with a sword and one with an axe. Jovian parried the sword thrust and then just ducked the axe swing that followed immediately after, but he doubted he'd be able to do that again, as he was weakening rapidly from blood loss. Feinting with his gladius in an effort to keep them at bay, Jovian slowly backed away until he was alongside the scorpio, hoping to put that between him and them. By doing so, he hoped that he would only have to face one of them at a time, but they saw what he was trying to do and rushed him.

This time he managed to block the axe blow with his gladius, though the strength it took to do so sent ripples of pain down his arm. Meanwhile the other warrior had managed to find an opening, and Jovian screamed as his sword plunged into his shoulder a finger's breadth from where the arrow still protruded. The pain was intense. Mustering all his remaining strength, he thrust forward with his gladius and was satisfied to feel the unmistakeable resistance of flesh and bone as his blade plunged into the other man's guts.

Too weak to fight anymore, he released his grip on his gladius and waited for the axeman to send him to Elysium. He and his band of wounded men had put up a valiant defence and bought the legate and his men some time to escape. He just hoped that it was enough. Farther along the rampart, he could see that his men had done as he'd instructed and set fire to the scorpio to save it falling into enemy hands. He just wished he had the energy to do the same to the one against which he now leaned. Instead, he closed his eyes and awaited death.

"Get up, Centurion Jovian. Nobody gave you permission to die yet."

Jovian reluctantly opened one eye. He was content and had accepted his death was imminent. Who was demanding yet more of him? His gaze fell on the chief surgeon. The man was actually grinning. Covered in blood and gore from head to foot, he looked like a monster from the lowest reaches of Tartarus, not a man more used to saving lives than taking them.

"You're still alive?" said Jovian.

"Yes, and so are you, so on your feet and die like a Roman. That's an order."

Jovian accepted his extended hand and then retrieved his gladius from the guts of the warrior he had just killed. "I think your talents might have been wasted in the medical profession."

"We all do what we can," the chief surgeon replied.

"The scorpio…" began Jovian.

"Don't worry. I'm taking care of it." As he spoke, the chief surgeon used all his strength to push the machine from the rampart and it smashed on the ground below. Several warriors who had narrowly missed being crushed, looked up angrily and began to make their way towards the two men. "I think we may soon have company."

"Good. Let's end this," replied Jovian, "while I can still stand."

Around them the sounds of battle had ended, other than the odd cry of pain from a wounded man. Even those were diminishing as warriors wandered round the fort finishing off the wounded, their own men included.

Jovian and the chief surgeon looked about them. The fight was indeed over; the fort had fallen. About ten paces behind them stood a group of six warriors, murder in their eyes. In front of them stood a slightly larger group, containing the men from the square below.

"Looks like this is it, Centurion," said the chief surgeon as the two men turned back to back so that each confronted one group of enemy warriors.

"It does. You and your men should be proud," said Jovian. "You all fought well."

"Was it worth it, I wonder?"

Jovian didn't reply. He was too weak, too tired.

"Throw down your weapons and surrender!" called a large warrior in faltering Latin from down in the fort square. "I will spare your lives."

"Like Hades you will!" Jovian watched as a familiar face came and stood by the warrior who was talking. He recognised him as somebody who had been with Corvo and his men when he had first met them. "You … you're one of Corvo's men."

"I was never one of his men. I merely used him to gain my freedom and return to my people."

"Be sure to tell him that just before he cuts your throat. Nobody likes a traitor," replied Jovian.

"Well, you won't be there to witness it, Roman."

"Enough! Last chance, Centurion! Throw down your weapons and I will spare your lives. As chieftain of this war band, I swear it."

"You ready?" Jovian whispered to the chief surgeon.

"I am."

"I'm already as good as dead, so if you want my weapons you're going to have to come and take them!" shouted Jovian.

The chieftain laughed. "As you wish." He nodded at one of the warriors on the ramparts and with a roar, the two groups charged at the Romans.

Jovian and the chief surgeon met the charge with roars of their own and swung their weapons. The chief surgeon managed to run one man through with his gladius and stuck his fingers deep into the eyes of another warrior, before four blades punched into his flesh and he slipped silently to the ground, the blind man's howls of pain the last thing he ever heard.

Jovian had managed to slice his gladius into the neck of one warrior; it wasn't an immediate kill, but the man was as good as dead. Numerous blades had pierced his flesh and as he felt the world start to drift away from him, in one last act of defiance, Jovian managed to grab two of the warriors who had attacked him. Roaring, he pushed them off the rampart, and they all crashed to the ground.

Jovian lay next to them, staring up at the sky, his field of vision shrinking all the time. A shadow loomed over him and raised something high in the air, and then Centurion Vitus Jovian of the Twenty-Second Legion breathed no more.

CHAPTER 16

Sleep had not come easily for Corvo, nor the men with him. Since leaving Fort Felix the previous night, they had been marching for nearly twenty-four hours. By the time the legate had given the order to fall out, it was all the men could do to collapse to the ground. The journey had been tough so far and was only likely to get more difficult.

Upon leaving Fort Felix, they had walked alongside the Rhenus for as long as possible before veering off into the relative safety of the forest as dawn broke. Space had become limited as the trees became more and more dense, meaning that their column had to stretch. This in turn made them more vulnerable to attack and less able to protect themselves, as their best chance of survival was to stick close together.

Consequently the journey was slow, much slower than Corvo liked, and it was not until mid-morning on their first day that they passed Fort Otto, or the smouldering remains of what was left of it. From the perceived safety of the trees, the column solemnly made its way past the fort, now a burned husk of the bastion it used to be. The tribesmen had gone there in force after their scouts reported seeing the garrison leave, perhaps hoping to catch them up and destroy the Romans on the march, but as Corvo had planned, they had been too late, and the garrison had already linked up with its brother units at Fort Felix. After no doubt plundering the fort, though there would have been little of value left for them, the tribesmen had vented their fury by setting fire to the fort, clearly hoping to stop the Romans from ever being able to occupy their lands again.

When are these people going to realise that when Rome plants a legionary's sandal in the ground, that ground becomes Roman territory, and the legions never leave? Corvo wondered.

The Germani warriors under the traitor Arminius fifty years earlier had believed that their total destruction of three Roman legions under the command of General Varus would be enough to persuade the Romans to leave Germania north of the Rhenus. They had been wrong, because Rome never forgot and never forgave, and five years after the ambush in the Teutoburg Forest, Germanicus had returned and avenged Varus.

When the Romans woke from a fitful and unrefreshing sleep on that second day since leaving Fort Felix, it was cold and damp. The sky, not that they could see much of it through the dense canopy of leaves high above, was grey, threatening more rain or even snow. The men ate a light meal washed down with ice-cold water or watered-down wine. Nobody laughed or joked. There was a collective nervousness pervading the camp, which didn't go unnoticed by Corvo or the legate.

"Morale is low this morning, Legate," said Corvo as he and the other officers not on watch sat around a small campfire. The legate had been reluctant to permit fires, even small ones, but both Gemmellus and Vortrix had assured Corvo that the smoke from these fires was unlikely to be spotted, as there was no high ground around them. If the tribesmen smelled it, they were already too close to their column and they were probably doomed anyway. It wasn't an encouraging reading of the situation, but it had been enough to persuade the legate to allow the fires. Corvo also reckoned that by doing so, they may have saved some lives.

"I'm not surprised. A long march through never-ending forests in wet and cold conditions with a horde of murderous barbarians on their trail was never going to engender good spirits," the legate grumbled.

"How much farther to the Claudian bridge?" Flavius asked.

"Between two and three days' march, so Gemmellus tells me. Depends on the terrain and the speed we move at, of course," replied Corvo.

"Not to mention the possibility that we might be attacked at any moment," added Tribune Crispus.

"Is that likely?" asked Flavius.

"I think we should assume that by now Fort Felix has fallen and the comrades we left behind have perished. The tribesmen's scouts will have found our tracks and if they aren't already after us, then they soon will be," said the legate.

"And they know these forests better than us and will be moving faster than we could ever hope to," added Tribune Ortius.

"Which means there is every chance that they will catch up with us either later today or early tomorrow," the legate concluded.

"If they do, we'll just have to handle it," said Corvo, sounding more confident than he felt. "Anyway, it may not be as bleak as you all seem to think."

They all looked at him expectantly.

"And why is that, Centurion Corvo?" asked the legate.

"The Germani tribesmen are no different to our men, Legate, in that they like to plunder what they can when they capture an enemy town or camp."

"Yes, we know that, Corvo, but we have left nothing of value save for the weapons and armour they will be able to strip off our dead soldiers. That's not going to delay them long enough for us to make good our escape," the legate replied irritably.

"But that's where you're wrong, Legate," said Corvo daringly, and the legate shot him a warning look. "The silver we could not carry — I didn't have it all buried or hidden."

"Oh?"

"No. I got some of the men digging holes before we left — some inside the fort, some outside. Some have got coins in, but the tribesmen won't know which ones and will have to dig them all up, which will take some time. More has been hidden within the fort. They'll have to tear the place apart before they'll be satisfied that they haven't missed any."

"So let me get this right, Centurion Corvo: instead of protecting the emperor's silver and hiding it securely out of reach of the tribesmen, you've left some lying around in open view and hidden the rest in some sort of treasure hunt for them?"

"I would argue that the silver was no longer the emperor's and belonged to the legionaries, sir, but yes — that sums it up. Oh, and I may have left in easy view the fort's entire wine supply, save for what the men are carrying."

"I see, so they are now drunk and rich," said the legate. Corvo waited for the rebuke he was sure was coming, but the legate went on, "Brilliant, Corvo, brilliant. It just might be the difference between us making the bridge or not. The chieftain will have little chance of reining in all but his most loyal warriors until they're sure they've found everything. Well done, Corvo. Well, I suggest we make the most of this opportunity Corvo's given us and break camp immediately. Agreed?" All the officers huddled around the fire nodded their agreement. "Good, we move out as soon as the fires are extinguished."

The legate stood up and strode off to relieve himself, shaking his head in amusement.

It was not until a little after noon on the third day that contact with the enemy was made. Flavius and the men bringing up the rear of the column all claimed to have seen or heard something behind them and on their flanks earlier that morning, but no attack had materialised. The legate had started to hope that it was tiredness and nerves causing the men to see danger where none existed. That was the case right up until one of the legionaries bringing up the rear was struck by an arrow.

The order was immediately given to shelter behind their shields, and the legionaries quickly squatted down and formed two long lines of interlocked shields. They had done so quickly and efficiently, but there had still been time enough for some arrows and spears to find flesh. Even when the defensive formation was in place, there were still gaps that a lucky shot or throw could penetrate.

The attack was neither protracted nor intense, and it was not long before the legate gave the order to stand. Corvo glanced around and saw that perhaps a score of men lay dead or injured. Those with leg wounds so severe that they couldn't stand or walk were bid a solemn goodbye by their comrades and left to take their own lives. Those who had only suffered minor wounds were quickly bandaged. Only one enemy warrior lay dead, courtesy of an arrow shot by the Syrian archer Kochar.

"Not an equitable exchange of casualties," the legate bemoaned when Corvo came to join him.

"No, and not one we can afford to repeat very often."

"Why didn't they press home their attack, do you think?"

"Most likely this is just a scouting party sent on ahead by the chieftain. They obviously decided to grab a bit of glory for themselves by attacking us and then telling their friends back at the camp."

The legate nodded his agreement. "Yes, I think you're probably right. The question is, how do I prevent them from doing this?"

"I don't think there is anything we can do, Legate. We need to keep moving. If we start to play cat and mouse with them, we are just going to be delayed. The longer we're out here doing that, the longer they've got to bring their whole war band up. We must remain vigilant, but I'm afraid we are going to sustain losses. Their scouts will be delayed by their desire to loot our fallen."

"I think you are probably right, Centurion, but let us hope that should we be fortunate enough to reach the Claudian bridge and it is still intact, we have men left who will need to cross it," said the legate, and Corvo nodded. "Get them moving again, Centurion."

The next attack came about an hour later, this time from their right flank. Centurion Galba had spotted a flicker of movement behind a tree and had bellowed the order to assume defensive formation, not waiting for the legate's order. His expediency saved many lives, and the Roman casualties when the attackers again melted away into the trees, were only six. Three tribesmen had also been killed, one by an arrow from Kochar and two by pilums. When they were sure the enemy had retreated far enough, the legionaries were allowed to go and retrieve their pilums.

The third and final attack of the day came just as the light was fading. Having already been assaulted from the rear and right flank, the legate had gambled that the next attack would come from their left flank. The men were on high alert to not only repel any attack from that direction, but also to launch what he hoped would be a deadly barrage of pilums in a counter-attack.

The legate was proved right and when the last attack of the day did come, it was from the Romans' left flank. Their attackers had barely got off any arrows before a deadly volley of pilums headed their way. In truth, with their bowmen spread out and often firing from behind trees, most of the pilums failed to find a target, either embedding themselves in trees or falling harmlessly to the ground. Yet others did and while the number of Germani casualties was still very low, the legate hoped that the fact they were able to anticipate and repel the tribesmen's attack would be enough to give them pause. Next time they attacked, he suspected it would be in far greater numbers and not from a predictable position.

"That should make them think again," said the legate, beaming as he saw Corvo and his son walking towards him.

"It will make them more cautious," replied Corvo. "The men are retrieving their pilums as we speak."

"Good. Well, we'll stop here for the night," said the legate. Corvo and Tribune Crispus looked around them, and their expressions told the legate what they thought of his decision. "I know, but I can't risk sending Gemmellus ahead to scout for a better place, not in this failing light. They already know where we are, so there's nothing to be gained by struggling a short way further. I doubt they will trouble us again today."

A piercing scream rang through the trees and the legionaries immediately took up defensive positions behind their shields as the officers tried to assess where the screaming was coming from.

"Have they managed to catch one of our men?" asked the legate.

"I don't believe so. They haven't come close enough to attempt it, and all our scouts are accounted for. Can anyone tell where that screaming is coming from?" shouted Corvo.

"In there, Centurion," a middle-aged legionary with a heavily scarred right arm said as he used his gladius to indicate the direction of the cries.

Corvo nodded and after telling Flavius to follow him with four legionaries, he jogged off to investigate. No more than twenty or so paces inside the trees to their left, he found the source of the screaming. Two legionaries who had gone to retrieve their pilums had fallen into a pit the depth of a man, at the bottom of which were a number of sharpened wooden stakes. One legionary was slumped face down, impaled on two stakes, one through his chest and one through his thigh. The man was clearly dead. The other legionary, the one who was screaming so pitifully, had fallen into the pit backwards and the stake had gone in through his lower back and emerged through what was left of the man's groin area.

Corvo heard one of the legionaries behind him vomit, and he thought he might do the same. Not only was the sight of the impaled men nauseating, but there was also a vile smell coming from the pit.

"Dear Mithras," whispered Flavius when he looked down at the pitiful sight in front of him, "what do we do?"

"We don't have any medical staff with us. They all remained at Felix and are most probably dead by now, and even if we did, what could they do for him? Even if we could get him out, the infection would kill him in a few days. That smell — they've smeared the stakes in human excrement."

"Bastards!" Flavius spat. "So what do we do? His screaming will bring curious warriors here to investigate."

Corvo leaned past his friend and tried to tug a pilum free of a legionary's grasp. The man didn't seem to notice at first; his gaze was fixed on the horror below him. He gradually relaxed his grip until Corvo was able to take the pilum.

Corvo hefted the javelin in his right hand and glanced down at the screaming man below. He knew he had to put him out of his misery. He was just glad that because of the arch of the man's back, he was not looking up and didn't know what was coming. Corvo drew his arm back and threw. The pilum struck the legionary squarely in the chest, killing him instantly.

Corvo turned to the legionary he had taken the pilum from. "Find yourself another pilum, but be careful where you tread. We don't know how many more of these traps there are."

When Corvo returned to the column, the legate, Tribune Crispus and Centurion Galba were waiting for an update. Tribune Ortius was at the rear of the column.

"What was it, Centurion?" asked the legate, eyeing Corvo's pale face.

"A pit filled with excrement-tainted stakes. Two men fell in. One was dead, one wasn't. Now they both are." Corvo didn't bother explaining how, and nobody asked.

"Are there more?" asked Tribune Crispus, glancing around nervously.

"Probably, but as for where they are, your guess is as good as mine. It just seems completely random to have one here in the middle of nowhere, but I expect the tribesmen know where they all are."

"Dear Mithras, we could fall into one at any moment," said Tribune Crispus.

"No, as long as we stay on what passes for a track, I believe we'll be all right. This was off to the side, farther inside the trees. My guess is that any others will be similarly located, though I'd encourage everybody to be extra vigilant. It is a horrific way to go."

"So now we've got to keep one eye on the trees and the other on the ground in front of us — how in Hades are we supposed to do that?" asked Flavius.

"I don't know, Lucius. It's worked out perfectly for the tribesmen. If we hurry, we increase the likelihood of falling into traps, but if we move slowly and carefully, their war band is going to catch up with us and we'll be slaughtered by them. There's no easy answer."

"Then tomorrow morning we carry on as we have been, moving as fast as we dare while remaining vigilant. The main host can't be far behind us now. These minor attacks have just been to harry us and delay us, nothing more. Once the main war band catches up, they will hit us with everything they've got in a place of their choosing, so we need to get to that bridge as soon as we can," said the legate.

"Assuming it's still there," added Tribune Crispus.

The Romans set up camp there for the night. No defensive ditches were dug and no earth ramparts were built, as was standard practice for a marching camp. Instead the men gathered around fires and relied on the large number of sentries the legate had ordered to warn them of any impending attack. The fires were greatly appreciated by the cold, tired and hungry legionaries. There was no point in worrying about whether the tribesmen could see them, as they already knew where they were and quite probably had for some time now. Sentries were rotated every two hours so that everyone had the chance to sleep. When the men needed to relieve themselves, they had to do so on the far edge of the camp, and to their amusement, they had to have a chaperone. Nobody was to go wandering into the forest in the dark. For once, none of the legionaries complained.

CHAPTER 17

Shortly after dawn, the enemy attacked again. This time, they came at the Romans from both sides at once, the sentries barely having time to shout a warning before the first arrows began peppering the legionaries. By the time Galba, Corvo and the others had cajoled the men into two shield walls, over a dozen legionaries were down. The attack was more prolonged and intense this time, but there was no mad rush of warriors pouring out of the trees. Instead the warriors seemed content to pick a few Romans off from afar while suffering minimal casualties themselves. Once the Romans had assumed their almost impenetrable defensive formation, the tribesmen retreated into the obscurity of the trees.

"On your feet!" barked the legate when he was convinced that the tribesmen had once again moved out of attack range. "Centurions Corvo and Galba, get these men moving. Leave everything but your weapons and water. Today we are going to move as quickly as we can and throw a little caution to the wind."

Corvo and Galba then started barking orders to the weary men, who sluggishly got to their feet and started forming a column. Corvo watched them and wondered whether the legate was expecting too much. They'd been marching for two days and two nights with minimal sleep while under the constant threat of attack, and nerves were fraught. He didn't know how much more some of the men had to give. He didn't know how much more he had to give.

The men had been travelling at the best speed their officers could drag out of them and were on the verge of stopping for a brief respite when the next attack came. Corvo almost welcomed it. The constant stress of watching and listening for the slightest movement or sound was starting to take its toll.

Again the tribesmen attacked with arrows and spears from both sides, and again the Romans suffered casualties before they were able to get into their defensive formations. This time, however, when the hail of missiles ceased, the tribesmen did not retreat. Instead, a horde of axe and sword-bearing warriors came running out of the trees from both flanks towards the Romans.

"Hold your position! Hold your line!" shouted Corvo and the other officers, and then the warriors slammed into the Romans.

This was what the Romans had been waiting for; this was what they had trained for day after day, week after week. So long as their lines held, they would cut the poorly protected barbarians to pieces.

The bravest of the Germani warriors hurled themselves at the Roman lines, their axes and swords crashing down into the implacable wall of shields. Then, when an opportunity presented itself, a gladius would flick out between the shields to pierce guts and groins before being quickly withdrawn, and the gap in the shield wall closed.

Still the Germani raged on. Here and there they enjoyed success. An axe head sunk into the top of a shield and then pulled it back, leaving a Roman's chest and neck exposed. A tribesman then quickly thrust his sword into the vulnerable Roman before trying to breach the gap and force his way through. The Romans were well versed in this type of fighting, though, and as soon as the man in the front row went down, his body was dragged out of the way, into the heart of the defensive formation, and a man from the second rank seamlessly took his place.

Corvo stood behind the two lines with Atilus at his side, watching the battle and roaring orders and encouragement to his men. The lines were holding and the Romans were only suffering minimal casualties, while the bravest and the toughest of the chieftain's warriors were dying by the dozen.

Corvo watched as a large, bare-chested tribesman with a two-handed war axe used the bodies of his dead comrades as a springboard and managed to leap over the front rank of legionaries. He clattered into the second rank, sending both himself and two legionaries crashing to the ground. For a big man he was exceptionally fast, and he was on his feet in a heartbeat. Atilus moved to intercept the warrior, but before he could, two legionaries in the second rank turned to face the warrior, clearly worried about being attacked from behind. Both legionaries rushed him at the same time, but the tribesman merely swung his axe as powerfully as he could at waist height. It smashed into one legionary's shield, splitting it in two, before knocking the shield out of the other legionary's hand. Shocked at how easily their only defence had been dispensed with, the two legionaries hesitated. The tribesman didn't. Bringing his axe round in another seemingly effortless arc, the warrior crashed it into the head of the legionary on the right, slicing through his helmet and into his skull, while he used his left leg to push the other legionary to the ground. By the time the man had regained his footing, the warrior had managed to tug his axe free, leaving the dead legionary's head split open in a gory mess of blood and brains.

The second legionary had stared at the grisly sight for too long, and by the time he managed to drag his horrified gaze away, the tribesman's axe was already nearing his own head. It smashed into his mouth, sending teeth flying and breaking his jaw. Moments later, the axe blade sliced into his midriff. When the tribesman pulled his blade free, the man's guts started to spill out after it.

The tribesman roared his battle cry as he glanced around for his next target, just in time to see a pilum hurtling towards him. Showing astonishingly quick reflexes, the warrior was able to safely deflect its trajectory with his axe shaft. The point instead struck another legionary in his calf, sending him to the ground, howling.

Atilus had seen enough. He planted himself in front of the tribesman, immediately catching his attention. The tribesman eyed him, seemingly taking in his long hair and his lack of armour and helmet. Holding a gladius in his right hand and a javelin in his left, Atilus closed in on the tribesman. They circled one another slowly, oblivious to the fighting going on around them. Eventually the warrior tired of the preamble and swung for Atilus' head, which he easily ducked, before aiming the axe at knee height. Atilus nimbly jumped over it. The warrior was quick and strong, but Atilus had bested many a man in the arena whom he shouldn't have. He knew that brawn and speed would only get him so far; brains and skill would keep him alive. Having both helped.

They circled one another again for a few moments, and then Atilus went on the offensive. He thrust the javelin towards the warrior's right side, inflicting a glancing blow as the man managed to twist his body at the last moment. But this movement left his left side vulnerable, and so Atilus was able to thrust in his gladius.

The tribesman howled. Then, as Atilus tried to pull his gladius free, he headbutted the former gladiator, sending him stumbling backwards and crashing to the ground. Atilus' gladius dropped from his grasp but landed a couple of paces away from him.

The pain in Atilus' head was blinding and he felt nauseous, but even as he hit the ground he knew that if he remained still, he was dead. Ignoring the pain as best he could, he rolled quickly to his left. The axe struck the wet ground a couple of moments later and Atilus immediately repeated his movement, this time rolling to his right. Again he heard the wet thud of an axe striking the muddy ground, followed by the frustrated grunt of the tribesman. As he rolled to his right, Atilus had managed to reach for his fallen gladius, and in one fluid movement he grabbed it and swung low, biting deeply into the big warrior's left ankle. The tribesman howled again and tried to bring his axe down where Atilus lay, but Atilus moved once more. With a roar of anger, the warrior then collapsed to the ground.

Atilus was on his feet in a moment and retrieved his javelin. The warrior was furiously trying to get to his feet, but the tendons in his ankle were severed, rendering him helpless. He could see Atilus poised to strike with his javelin and repeatedly swung his axe in low arcs, trying to cut Atilus down, but the ex-gladiator was too agile and avoided every predictable swing. Gradually the big warrior tired and stopped swinging, ready to embrace the inevitable. Atilus stepped in close and drove the javelin into the tribesman's heart.

He stepped back, closed his eyes and tried to get his breathing back under control. It was only then that he realised that save for the odd pitiful wail of an injured or dying man, the area was now silent. He opened his eyes and saw just about every Roman, including the legate and Corvo, staring at him in admiration. It seemed the battle had been won while he was fighting, and the tribesmen had once again retreated.

Somewhere to Atilus' right, one of the men began to slowly chant his name. Another voice joined in, and then another, until eventually nearly every soldier was chanting his name. He closed his eyes once more and smiled as he recalled another time, a time when he would walk out onto the sands of the biggest arenas across the Empire and fight the best gladiators, none of whom were ever his match. Men had been envious, and women had lusted after him. A slave he may have been, but on those occasions when he'd stood on the sand he was a god. While he vowed he would never again be a slave, Atilus had to admit he missed those days sometimes.

"Shall I stop them?" Corvo asked the legate.

"No, let him have his moment. It is good that the men have something to cheer about; it will do their morale no harm."

"We're never going to hear the end of this, you know," said Galba, frowning. "The way he'll tell it is that he saved our entire column."

"He does love a tale," replied Corvo.

"Especially when he's the hero."

"Come on, let's go and rescue him before his head swells so much he cannot navigate the trees," said Corvo, smiling. But by the time they reached Atilus, the cheering and chanting had already started to die down. Atilus looked disappointed.

"Well fought, Atilus," said Corvo.

"Thank you. He was a fine warrior."

"Bit long in the tooth, if you ask me, and you made a meal out of him, playing to the crowd," said Galba, straight-faced. "While you were dancing with this old man, I, Corvo and the others were holding the entire war band off. You're welcome, by the way." Eventually, he could no longer hold it together, and both men burst out laughing.

"Then we'll call it even," said Atilus, grinning.

"No wonder you're in debt if that's your idea of even," muttered Galba. When Atilus had first asked to join Corvo's mission to Armenia, he had stated that he needed to leave Rome for a while because he owed money to some gangs in the Serpentine, though he never told them how much or why.

"What happened, anyway?" asked Atilus.

"Their chieftain must have realised they were taking too many casualties and called them off. They'll be back, though. Gemmellus reckons we should make the Claudian bridge tomorrow morning," replied Corvo.

"Something I don't understand, Centurion: everybody seems to think that by just reaching the bridge, we'll be safe, but won't they just cross it and come after us?"

"Hopefully not, though I'll concede that it is a possibility. This side of the river has always largely been their territory, except for punitive expeditions and false alliances like those with Varus with Arminius. The other side is well and truly part of the Roman Empire. If they cross over that bridge in force, they would be risking full-scale war with us, and I don't think they will want that. But you're right — if the chieftain is angry enough he may order his warriors across, hoping that other tribes will rally to his cause if Rome attacks in force. But let's worry about that tomorrow."

"A fine contest, Atilus. Well done," said the legate, coming over to join them.

"Thank you, Legate. I'm glad somebody appreciates my talents."

"Quite. Time to move, I think, men." The legate turned to resume his place at the head of the column.

The order to move out was greeted with the usual groans from weary men, but they were soon once again moving north-west towards the Claudian bridge.

It was not until late that afternoon that the next attack happened. A large band of warriors had come pouring down the track behind them and attacked the rear of the Roman column, which was being commanded by Tribune Ortius. There had been no hail of arrows preceding this attack, and the Romans were caught in a column with only the men at the rear able to engage the enemy. By the time Centurion Galba had organised a support force to come and aid Tribune Ortius, the tribesmen were already receding back into the trees, leaving a number of dead Romans in their wake. Among them was Tribune Ortius, who had put himself in the thick of the fighting like a true commander. As the tribesmen had retreated, Tribune Ortius had continued to organise his men and had been struck by three arrows fired by Germani archers who had materialised to cover their comrades' retreat. The tribune had been dead before he hit the ground.

"I begin to understand how Varus must have felt," said Legate Crispus as he watched the men check that all the fallen Romans were dead. Once again, those that weren't were helped on their way without preamble. It was telling that nobody protested now.

"We can't take much more of this, Legate," said Corvo.

"Nor do we need to. We should arrive at the bridge by mid-morning tomorrow, so Legionary Gemmellus assures me."

"Not a moment too soon. All we have to do now is survive the night and morning and hope that they don't pursue us over the bridge," said Corvo sarcastically. The legate gave him a disapproving look but said nothing.

"All the men have been taken care of, sir," said Galba, joining them. "Only had to help one of the men on his way."

"And Tribune Ortius?" asked the legate.

"Laid out with the rest of them, sir. The men say he fought like a man possessed, leading from the front."

"The man could be trying at times, but he was a true son of Rome and died like one. Thank you, Centurion. Post double guards and we'll stop here for the night; it's as good a place as any. We'll break camp before dawn tomorrow and make haste to the bridge. If the gods favour us, we'll manage to stay ahead of the war band."

The night passed peacefully, save for the howls of wolves, though Corvo wasn't entirely convinced they were wolves. As the legate had ordered, double guards were posted, and these were rotated several times during the night. Twice the men were called to stand-to, two different sentries having claimed they'd seen or heard something moving in the trees, but nothing materialised and no attack was forthcoming. The sentries responsible for calling the stand-to found themselves being roundly abused by their irate and exhausted comrades. Nobody truly slept that night.

Then, just as the sun was rising, the men were quietly roused from their slumber and given a short while to drink and relieve themselves before being ordered into a column. As silently as possible, they then slowly trudged out of their overnight camp, travelling north-west towards the Claudian bridge.

CHAPTER 18

Not long after the Romans had moved out, they heard a roar through the trees, sending crows into panicked flight. The men glanced at each other anxiously. There could be no doubt that the whole war band was on their trail now, not just a few warriors whose intention was to keep stinging the Roman column rather than force it into battle. Now things had changed. The tribesmen were also closer than the Romans had hoped, and those at the rear of the column would suffer first.

Centurion Galba saw the men's fear. Some of them looked ready to make a run for it. All it would take was for one man to start the trickle, and it would soon become a flood. Then they'd be lost. They had one chance to survive this, however slim: they needed to remember their training, stay disciplined and stick together.

"Steady now, men. Keep moving, hold your formation and we'll be fine." He only spoke loud enough for the men at the back of the column to hear, but they would be the men to break first, as it was only Galba himself between them and the war band closing in from behind.

They jogged on for a while longer, the need for silence and stealth now passed. All that mattered now was speed. The shouts and calls of the men chasing them were growing louder all the time. Without being ordered, the pace of the column picked up and to Galba's annoyance, the column began to lose its shape as the fitter and stronger men began to pull ahead. If it lost its shape it would lose its discipline, and then it would panic.

"Hold your position, damn you!" shouted Galba. His order had only really been intended for the men to the rear of the column, but his voice had carried all the way along the line. Slowly the column began to revert back to its original shape. Even Corvo and the legate had checked their pace and position upon hearing Galba's bellowed order, such was the authority it conveyed.

A short while later, the front of the column led by Corvo and the legate burst out of the trees into a clearing. As Corvo struggled to regain his breath, he looked about him and saw that about four hundred paces away, the Claudian bridge stood undamaged, spanning over the Rhenus.

"Legate!" The legate turned to look at Corvo, unable to respond for a moment as he struggled for breath. "The bridge — it's still there."

"Thank the gods." He turned and watched as the tail of the column emerged from the forest, the tall, bulky figure of Galba bringing up the rear. The big man didn't look out of breath at all.

As the men stood panting and drinking, Germani voices and shouts could be heard coming from the trees. They were almost upon them. Corvo realised that they were out of time and were going to have to fight. They had been so close. If they had been just a little earlier, they would have made it. If they tried to run now, he had no doubt that the tribesmen would fall on the backs of the rear of the column and slaughter would ensue. He glanced at the legate and saw that the same thoughts and doubts were on his mind.

"Form line! Form line!" bellowed Corvo, not waiting for the legate's orders. The cry was immediately taken up by the other officers, and the men began to wearily form a long line with their backs to the bridge.

By the time the line was formed, the first Germani warriors had burst out of the treeline. It took a few precious moments for their eyes to adjust from the gloom of the forest to the daylight, and Corvo and the other officers used that time to tighten the line and ensure that the shields were overlapping.

Corvo stood just left of the centre, with Flavius a few places to his left. The legate stood proudly and defiantly at the centre, with his son by his side. A few paces to their right stood Atilus the gladiator. Galba stood towards the end of the left wing, Optio Valens at the opposite end. They were painfully few and the Germani horde in front of them was many. More were emerging from the trees all the time.

Corvo glanced to his left and his eyes met those of Flavius. Neither spoke, but both understood this was probably the end. Corvo forced a small smile as he adjusted his helmet for what felt like the hundredth time, and Flavius merely shrugged before turning his attention back to the men in front of him.

"That's a lot of warriors, Legate," called Atilus, grinning.

"It is, Atilus, plenty to go round, so try not to be too greedy, eh?" This drew laughter from the men who heard.

"No promises."

"There's a lot of them, men, but I'd back any man from either the Twenty-Second or The Damned to be worth ten of them. Nobody is given permission to die until they've killed at least ten of the enemy, do I make myself clear?" shouted the legate.

"Yes, sir!" the men roared back in unison before laughing once again.

The tribesmen were working themselves up into a battle rage just across the clearing, an action meant to intimidate the Romans. The legate was having none of it.

"I can't hear you!" he roared at the top of his voice.

"Yes, sir!" the men roared back again even louder.

"Better. Courage and honour, men."

"Courage and honour," his men repeated.

A rhythmic banging of the gladius on the iron rim of a shield started at the far left of the line, and Corvo imagined it had been instigated by Galba. It soon spread along the line and became a deafening sound, one that had been used for hundreds of years to intimidate the enemy. Corvo was pleased to note that the shouts and roars of the barbarian host had subsided somewhat. The lull did not last long, however, and urged back into a frenzy by their leaders, the tribesmen were soon once again screaming and hurling insults at the Romans.

"Get ready, men. I think they've finally found the courage to come and die on our steel. Let's not disappoint them!" called Centurion Galba, making all of those who heard him laugh.

Then the tribesmen came. There was no order to their attack — they just charged at the Roman line in one mass, the quickest and bravest leading the way. Unlike the Romans, who always ensured optios were behind the lines to make sure nobody ran or broke formation, the Germani did not bother. Consequently, those whose courage was not as steadfast as their comrades' could more easily hang back without fear of punishment from behind.

The Roman line shook and in some places it bent as the leading warriors hurled themselves at it fearlessly. Most were immediately cut down as sharp steel flicked out from behind the wall of shields. Sometimes the gladii would appear over the top of the shield to sink into the neck or chest of the warrior in front. Other times the legionaries would part their shields and thrust their gladii into the groin or stomach of their enemy before hastily closing the gap. This was how the legions preferred to fight, and they were good at it. Lethally good, and the Germani dead were soon piling up in front of them, though the tribesmen were not without success. Here and there a legionary had been killed or wounded, but before the line could be breached, one of the men who had hurled the javelins from the rear quickly stepped in to fill the gap. Aside from the half dozen archers, there were only three javelin throwers now free to plug any further gaps that might appear. They were now busy dragging the severely wounded away from the line so that when the order to pull back was given, their comrades did not stumble over them.

A horn sounded and apart from three or four warriors whose blood was clearly up, the tribesmen disengaged and began to walk back to their own lines, safe in the knowledge that the Romans' supply of javelins was clearly exhausted and that they wouldn't be cut down by a deadly hail. Some of the warriors had the sense to pick up the javelins that had been thrown in case the Romans tried to retrieve them. For some that meant pulling the weapons from the bodies of their fallen friends and family. They turned and taunted the Romans with their prizes as they slowly withdrew.

The three or four warriors who had not heeded the call to retreat soon found themselves outnumbered and were quickly cut down.

"Dress that line!" barked Centurion Galba as the men sought to rest their aching arms by grounding their shields. A cry of pain echoed along the line as a legionary was punched backwards by a pilum thrown by a retreating tribesman. It had slammed into his chest, killing him instantly. "Dress that line now, damn you!" The men hurriedly raised their shields once again, forming what they hoped would be an impenetrable line. "Legionary Servius?"

"Centurion?" responded the young soldier who had joined their ranks after the battle at Fort Lipa in Armenia. He was one of the three men tasked with dragging the severely wounded to the rear, having thrown his pilum, a weapon with which he had proved proficient.

"Are you dead or dying?"

"No, Centurion," replied Servius, almost guiltily.

"Then what are you doing standing there like a virgin in a brothel? Join the line where that other fool was. And keep your shield up."

"Yes, Centurion," replied Servius as he watched the fallen legionary's body being dragged out of the way by his two comrades.

"At least we've got a javelin now. That should make a difference, right?" said Flavius. Corvo looked at him but didn't reply. "I suppose not, then."

"Line will withdraw fifty paces in good order!" bellowed the legate. Immediately the line pulled back, almost in step with one another.

The Romans' withdrawal didn't go unnoticed, and a roar emanated from within the tribesmen's ranks. Moments later, the host raced towards the Roman line again.

"Brace!" shouted Corvo and Galba at the same time as once again the tide of warriors smashed into their shield wall, though the attack looked a little less enthusiastic this time. The few pilums the tribesmen had managed to retrieve were hurled as they ran, and only two of these found flesh, one killing a legionary outright, the other going right through the thigh of another. He would soon bleed out.

Again the deadly gladii flicked out from between and over the shields, piercing flesh almost without fail. In response, tribesmen's swords slammed futilely into the shields of the

Romans while those with war axes tried to hook their axe heads over the top of the shields and drag them down. Here and there along the Roman line this tactic was working as the increasingly exhausted legionaries struggled to find the strength to hold their shields up.

Corvo slammed his shield umbo into the snarling face of the warrior in front of him and as he stumbled back, he thrust his gladius into the man's belly. Before the warrior had fallen to the ground, another one was pushing past him to get at Corvo, the traverse crest on his helmet singling him out as an officer. His sword darted forward, and Corvo only just managed to get his shield back up in time. Instinctively he flicked his own gladius out from the right of his shield and felt it slice flesh. The warrior howled with pain but renewed his attack. Three times he brought his sword crashing down towards Corvo, but each time it was met by Corvo's shield. Corvo was tiring, though, and realised that if the warrior didn't soon run out of energy and make a mistake, he could be in trouble.

The warrior suddenly took a couple of steps back and glanced down at his left thigh, which was awash with blood. Then, looking up, he saw Corvo grinning at him from above the rim of his shield. Incensed, the warrior threw himself at Corvo, another flurry of blows slamming futilely into the Roman's shield. The exertion and the loss of blood had taken its toll, however, and the warrior again stepped back, but this time he did not retreat far enough. Quick as lightning, Corvo's gladius shot out and pierced the man's left side. As Corvo pulled his sword free, another gladius blade stabbed into the warrior just below his right shoulder. A look of shock crossed the warrior's face and he collapsed to the ground just as the horn sounded once again and the tribesmen began to pull back once more.

Corvo glanced to his left and saw that Flavius was now the man next to him, all the others having been killed or wounded.

"Thought you might need help."

"I had it under control. I was just letting him tire himself out."

"If you say so," smirked Flavius. "Looks like we've earned another breather." He nodded towards the retreating tribesmen. "Surely they can't keep this up." Flavius was looking at the carpet of dead and dying bodies in front of them. To their left a tribesman screamed as a Roman gladius put him out of his misery.

"No, but neither can we," replied Corvo, glancing around at the dead Roman soldiers. "They'll pay a high price if they keep this up, but they will prevail."

"We were so close, so damn close," said Flavius bitterly as he shook his head.

"Fall back fifty paces in good order!" shouted the legate, but it was Galba's booming voice repeating the order which motivated the exhausted legionaries to begin to move.

"You never know — maybe a couple of us will make it to the bridge at this rate," said Flavius caustically.

Flavius and Corvo began to back away in step with their comrades. When they had gone perhaps twenty paces, Corvo almost tripped over a badly wounded soldier. His stomach was covered in blood and he was obviously in a great deal of pain.

"Brother ... please ... send me on my way... I can't..."

Before he could finish his request, Corvo had driven his gladius into the man's heart, ending his pain. He momentarily locked eyes with Flavius but neither man spoke, both knowing that he had done the right thing.

Corvo hurried to catch up with the retreating line and resumed his place. Elsewhere, other men were easing the passing of their badly wounded comrades.

When the Romans had retreated fifty paces and had still not been attacked by the tribesmen, the legate gave the order to keep moving back. By the time they were just two hundred and fifty paces from the bridge, the tribesmen had closed to within twenty paces and seemed to have worked themselves up into a battle fury again.

"Halt and lock shields!" bellowed the legate, but before the last shield had slotted into position the tribesmen had attacked.

Sensing that this was perhaps their last opportunity to crush the Romans without having to pursue them over the bridge, the tribesmen launched into their attack with renewed vigour and the Roman line shook under the weight and ferocity of their onslaught.

The tired Romans, greatly reduced in number, met their attack with a defiant stoicism.

Corvo stabbed the first man who appeared in front of him in the neck before using his shield to shove the dying man backwards. Another soon appeared and his sword darted over the top of Corvo's shield, aiming for his face. Corvo ducked low behind his shield before swinging it out of the way and thrusting his gladius deep into the man's groin. Once his gladius was pulled free, he immediately moved his shield back into position. The mortally wounded warrior cried out in agony and dropped his weapon, doubling over. The warrior behind him, a big man with a long, unkempt beard with more grey than brown, roughly grabbed his comrade by the tunic and pulled him out of the way.

He stood there for a moment or two, safely out of stabbing range, and glanced from Corvo to Flavius as if weighing up who to attack. Apparently realising that Corvo was a senior officer and that his death would bring him more glory, the warrior grasped his war axe and swung it in an arc at head height with astonishing speed. Both Corvo and Flavius had to quickly duck behind their shields to avoid being decapitated. Something told Corvo that the man was going to repeat his attack with a backwards swing, hoping to catch Corvo's head as he once again looked up. He therefore remained below the rim of his shield and prayed that Flavius would do the same.

Corvo had been half right. The warrior did reverse his swing, but not at head height. Instead he swung his axe back at chest height, hoping to make contact with Corvo's shield, and that is exactly what happened. Corvo could immediately see what the warrior intended, but he was too exhausted to stop him. The warrior grinned as he violently tugged with his axe and Corvo's shield flew from his grasp. The warrior pulled back his axe, ready to launch another powerful swing aimed at Corvo's head. Keeping low, Corvo stepped towards the warrior. The axe swing was so powerful that Corvo felt the air move and tickle the back of his neck as he stooped beneath its swing. Then he thrust forward with all his remaining strength, plunging his gladius as deeply into the man's stomach as he could. He heard the warrior grunt, and Corvo grasped the handle of his gladius with both hands and used all his strength to lever the blade backwards and forwards, making the wound ever wider.

The warrior roared with pain and rage. Dropping his axe, his left hand shot out like a cobra and grabbed Corvo about the throat. The man was dying, yet still seemingly had the strength to take Corvo with him. Panic began to grasp Corvo as black spots clouded his vision. While his left hand struggled to remove the warrior's hand from his throat, Corvo let go of his gladius and reached down to his waist. After a few moments his hand suddenly touched the handle of his pugio, a small dagger carried by all Roman soldiers.

With one final effort, Corvo managed to wrap his fingers around the pugio and pulled it free. Forcing his eyes to focus on the man before him, he brought the pugio up and repeatedly stabbed the big warrior in the neck. For a few long moments it looked as if even this wasn't going to defeat the warrior, but then one of his stabs found the big artery in the man's neck and hot blood began to spurt out. The effect was instantaneous. The tribesman let go of Corvo, then collapsed face down on the blood-soaked ground. Corvo crumpled to the ground, fighting for breath.

Corvo had no idea how long he'd been unconscious before he felt the rough hands of Centurion Galba on his shoulders.

"This is no time to be taking a nap, Centurion. You'll miss all the fun," he heard the big man say as his eyes reluctantly opened.

"I thought we'd lost you then," he heard Flavius say.

Corvo turned his head slightly and saw Flavius and the legate.

"You still in the fight, Centurion?" asked the legate.

"You mean we haven't won yet?" asked Corvo as his eyesight began to return to normal, as did his breathing.

"I'm afraid not, Centurion, though they seemed to lose heart when you put that big man down. Their courage quickly deserted them, and they ran away again," explained the legate.

"I don't suppose they kept running all the way back to their forest, did they?"

"No, more's the pity. They're gathered over there, what's left of them, no doubt trying to work up the courage to launch yet another attack. You'd think they'd have had enough by now. I almost admire their bravery. There's not many of them left, so the chieftain is going to have to lead the attack this time and commit his bodyguard. This will be the last battle for sure … one way or another."

"There aren't too many of us left either, sir," said Galba, his voice betraying no sign of panic or fear.

"I know. But I'd still back us, even though we're hopelessly outnumbered."

Corvo and the others glanced around and saw just how few they really were. The legate's words of encouragement were just that — words. Nobody there believed that they could possibly prevail against another enemy attack. There were just too many of them. But the tribesmen had paid a high price for the chieftain's fury and would continue to do so if they launched another attack. The chieftain had sacrificed the cream of his menfolk already and was clearly prepared to see every last man in his tribe killed if it meant he could take revenge for the rape of his wife and the murder of his son.

Once again Corvo found himself cursing Traianus for his horrific actions back in the enemy village — actions that could cost every Roman his life. Although they had never found Traianus' body after he'd fled the camp, Corvo was sure the man had to be dead. He found himself hoping that the traitor had suffered a grisly, painful demise. It would go some small way to atoning for what had transpired here.

"Looks like they're getting ready to attack again, Legate," said the legate's son.

"Thank you … Tribune," said the legate, smiling proudly. "Centurion Galba…"

"Sir?"

"Have the men form a square on the double."

"Yes, sir. Right, you lot, on your feet and form a square … now. The Empire hasn't finished with you yet."

Slowly and with much complaining, the remaining legionaries got to their feet and started to form a square.

"Legionary Thraxus, would you like me to send a message over to those barbarians to ask them if they wouldn't mind delaying their attack until you're ready? No? Then move yourself!" He cast his eye over to where the remaining men were attempting to form a square and rolled his eyes. "What in Hades' name is that supposed to be? I said form a square, so do it now! Straighten those lines." The chastened men did as they were told. "Better. Curse and hate me all you like, but you'll thank me when that lot come screaming over here shortly."

Corvo had watched the exchange from where he was still sitting and smiled ruefully. Thank the gods for centurions like Galba.

"Well, don't just stand there — give me a hand up," Corvo said to Flavius, and his friend extended a hand and pulled him up. It took Corvo a moment to regain his balance.

"You might need this," said Tribune Crispus, smiling and holding out Corvo's gladius, having retrieved it from the dead warrior's guts.

"Thank you, Tribune. You're right — it may just come in useful."

Another huge roar went up from where the remaining tribesmen were gathered.

"Sooner than you think, I would say," said Tribune Crispus, handing the gladius over as the two men went to join the square.

The enemy were racing towards them with all their fury.

The final battle was upon them.

CHAPTER 19

"You stand and hold!" shouted the legate. Nobody answered — there wasn't time. Instead they adjusted their grip on their gladii and braced their feet. Moments later, the horde of tribesmen smashed into their square, sending a shudder down the lines. Once again the shield walls around the square wavered but did not break.

"Hold them!" Corvo heard someone shout, but he couldn't tell who. Neither did it matter. Like every other legionary left standing, Corvo braced his feet, put his shoulder behind his shield and pushed back. The tribesmen's swords and axes thudded into the Romans' shields while others tried to drag the shields away with their axes, but the line held. The tribesmen's frustration began to grow as they failed to penetrate the square, and when Corvo finally felt the ferocity of the attack ease a little, he moved his shield to the left and thrust his gladius out. It bit deeply into flesh and Corvo immediately withdrew his gladius as the man crumpled to the ground.

Another warrior instantly took his place, a big man with gold torques that signified he was an important member of the tribe. His sword smashed into Corvo's shield three times, sending jolts of pain down the Roman's already aching arm. Then, either out of frustration or because he suddenly noticed an opening, the warrior drove his sword at the man to Corvo's left. Corvo felt hot blood spray the left side of his face as the warrior roared in triumph.

Corvo remembered that Flavius had been standing to his left earlier, and he feared that the big warrior had just killed his best friend, but there was no time to check. In reaching over to attack the man to Corvo's left, the warrior had exposed his left side. Corvo took the opportunity that presented itself and smashed his shield into the man's face, then drove his gladius into the warrior's side. The tribesman collapsed to the ground on top of the other warrior Corvo had killed just moments before. The gold torques on his forearm would make nice trophies for anybody who survived the slaughter.

Corvo just had time to glance around before another warrior appeared in front of him. While the square for the most part was holding, in a few places the enemy had broken through. The legate, Tribune Crispus and four other men the legate had chosen to form a reserve had quickly moved to intercept the tribesmen and prevent them from exploiting the breach. It was a noble effort but would ultimately be futile; the battle was already lost. All they could do now was die with honour and take as many of the enemy with them as they could.

A sword smashed into Corvo's shield, dragging him back to the moment. He just managed to raise it high enough to protect his head as a second blow came slicing in. Again Corvo used all his remaining strength to hammer his shield umbo into the tribesman's face. There was a sickening crunch as the man's nose was shattered, and he screamed in pain before reaching up to cup his ruined face. The moment he did, Corvo thrust his gladius forward, stabbing the man in the centre of his chest. He then pushed the dead man's body away from him with his foot as he pulled his gladius free.

Suddenly, somebody shouted that the square had been breached and the men were to slowly fall back to the bridge. Corvo risked another quick glance behind him and was alarmed to find that some tribesmen were indeed to their rear, having broken through the square at several points. The shield walls had all but disintegrated now and the remaining legionaries either fought on in small clusters or individually. In both cases, his men found themselves hopelessly outnumbered.

A mighty roar startled Corvo and he turned just in time to raise his shield to block an axe blow from one of the chieftain's bodyguards. The blow was so powerful that Corvo's shield finally splintered and fell from his hand as he collapsed to the ground. The warrior raised his axe again and chopped down towards Corvo's face, but he had anticipated the blow and rolled first to his left and then to his right when the warrior repeated his attack. As the warrior raised his axe once more, Corvo urgently cast his gaze about until he saw what he was looking for. Rolling to his right once again to avoid the latest downward axe chop, Corvo reached out and grabbed a fallen spear. The warrior was already raising his axe for another downward blow and as he did so, Corvo angled the spear towards the man's chest. The axe was already on its way down when the warrior realised his mistake, and the forward momentum of his attack carried him onto the spear point. The spear penetrated his chest by no more than a finger's length, but it was enough to make him let go of the axe. Corvo quickly spread his legs just in time, and the axe fell to the ground blade-first, a hand's length from his groin. Corvo stared at it wide-eyed for a moment in sheer relief.

The warrior was still very much alive, so Corvo grasped the spear shaft with both hands and pushed it deeper into the warrior's body, scrambling to his feet as he did so. The snarling warrior also grabbed the spear shaft and tried to push it out, but his strength was waning, and despite his exhaustion Corvo was the stronger of the two men. Soon the spear had been pushed so hard that the point protruded from the warrior's back. Corvo let go and the tribesman stumbled back a couple of paces. Still he lived. Corvo picked up his gladius and ran at him, slicing the man deeply across his neck. The big warrior stood there for a moment and then fell forwards. His body slowly slipped all the way down the spear shaft until he hit the ground, where he lay with the spear point and most of the shaft sticking out of his back.

Corvo quickly picked up a replacement shield from one of his fallen comrades and turned to face the next threat. Nobody immediately engaged him. There were many warriors in front of him, but they were all either looking behind them or to their left. It was then that Corvo saw what had drawn their attention — scores of arrows were dropping into the rear of the Germani horde.

"Pull back! Pull back to the bridge!" somebody shouted. Corvo was sure it was the legate. Slowly, the Romans began to stagger back while the tribesmen hesitated, unsure whether to press home the attack or retreat from the arrows which continued to pile into their rear ranks.

Corvo looked to his right and could have cried tears of joy. Across the river and in battle formation were hundreds of legionaries with scores of archers in front of them. The Twenty-Second, its banner fluttering in the wind and its standard gleaming brightly, had finally left the big fort across the Rhenus and come to their aid.

Shouting in front of Corvo drew his attention back to what was happening on his side of the river. He looked up to see what had to be the chieftain and some of his bodyguards, roaring and shouting at his men, some of whom had turned to run. A half dozen blades from the bodyguards sliced into the bellies of some of those who had thought to escape, and their comrades reluctantly turned to face the Romans once more for fear of suffering the same fate.

Then, with a final roar of encouragement from the chieftain, they charged towards Corvo and the other Romans who were still slowly backing away from them towards the bridge, which was now no more than forty paces away.

Just as Corvo and the others had resigned themselves to fighting and probably dying just paces from safety, another shout went up, this one in Latin. This time, Corvo didn't recognise the voice.

"Drop!"

Corvo immediately did as ordered and dropped into a crouch with his shield held over his head. Not everyone followed his example, either because they didn't hear the order or were just too exhausted to react. Moments later scores of javelins flew over their heads and slammed into the snarling mass of warriors just a few strides in front of them. Dozens of warriors dropped to the ground, dead or wounded, as did several Romans, including Optio Valens one of the men who Corvo had rescued along with the legate's son from the prison in Armenia. A spear had struck him in the lower back, killing him instantly. Sometimes the Fates could be cruel.

The tribesmen's attack faltered and when a second wave of javelins punched into their diminished ranks, it halted completely. The sensible and disciplined thing to do then was for the Romans to complete their retreat over the bridge to safety and let what remained of the Germani forces slink away into the forests. But that was not what happened. The legionaries' blood was up and they were furious about losing friends and comrades. Without waiting for orders, they surged forward to engage the startled tribesmen who had not yet had the good sense to run.

Corvo didn't know who made the first move and broke ranks. He was in no position to criticise their actions, given that he had done the same thing two years before — he had been forced to lead The Damned partly as a punishment. Whoever had made the first move had clearly not been alone in his thoughts, as nearly all of the remaining Romans on that side of the bridge joined him. Only the legate, Corvo, Galba and a few men too badly wounded to take part in any more fighting remained behind to observe what happened. The soldiers on the bridge and the other side of the river remained in position.

In front of Corvo a massacre was taking place. Out of the tribesmen who had taken part in the last charge, the chieftain and four of his bodyguards remained to face the Roman counter-attack. The others — old men who had seen too many summers and young boys who had not yet seen enough — had turned and run, their backs now easy targets for the vengeful Romans. No mercy was being shown and even as the tribesmen fled, discarding their weapons as they ran, they were being cut down without exception.

The gaze of the chieftain settled on the legate, Corvo and Galba. He said something to the men around him, and they all started to make their way towards Corvo's group.

Corvo weighed their chances. It was five against three, but that three included a senior officer past his prime, though the legate would never admit it. To his credit, the legate's courage did not falter as he took a step forward to meet the chieftain's challenge.

Unaware of the two groups about to square off, two Roman legionaries attacked two of the chieftain's bodyguards, but they were quickly and effortlessly despatched. These were the chieftain's best and toughest warriors, and Corvo knew then that the odds were most definitely stacked against them. He was just about to say so to the legate when two arrows from somewhere to their right struck the warrior on the end of the enemy line. One arrow pierced his left eye and the other his neck. The warrior dropped silently to the ground, but the chieftain didn't give his man a second glance. His gaze was fixed firmly on the legate.

Corvo was also suddenly aware that somebody had taken up position on his right, and he briefly glanced in that direction. He was relieved to see the grinning face of Atilus the gladiator alongside him. The numbers may now be equal, but to Corvo's mind, the odds had most definitely swung in their favour. Now he relished the fight to come. When the two groups were no more than seven or eight paces apart, the Germani charged.

The four Romans met them as one, but it was not long before four individual fights had broken out, with the legate being singled out by the chieftain while Corvo and the others faced off against his bodyguards. These were his elite warriors, the best his tribe had to offer.

Almost immediately, the Romans were put on the back foot, only Atilus standing his ground and matching his opponent. As career soldiers, Corvo, Galba and the legate had been taught and trained to fight in formation in a disciplined manner, whereas the tribesmen seemed content to always throw themselves headlong at the enemy and engage them in single combat.

The man facing Corvo was nothing short of a giant even by Germani standards, and he stood a good head taller than his opponent. He was also broad-shouldered and barrel-chested, and Corvo had no doubt that if the tribesman's sword made contact with his neck, his head would be sliced clean off.

Blow after blow rained down on Corvo's shield with no sign of the man tiring, though every muscle in Corvo's arm screamed with pain from the effort of keeping the shield up.

Whenever he could, Corvo slid his shield to the left and thrust out with his gladius, hoping to catch the warrior unaware. But like Corvo, this warrior was clearly a veteran of many battles, and he was always too quick.

More blows thundered against Corvo's shield and he began to worry that this one too might shatter. The tribesman suddenly changed tack, and his next swing was aimed at Corvo's neck. Corvo had seen something in the other man's eyes that had alerted him, but he had still only ducked just in time as the blade swept through the air, slicing the crest from his helmet. As the warrior prepared to bring his sword back around for another go, Corvo charged at him shield-first, keeping low and safely behind his shield as he did so. The shield crashed into the warrior's midriff and Corvo kept pushing forward, his momentum sending the warrior stumbling backwards. For a moment or two, it looked as if the big man was going to manage to stay upright, but eventually he tumbled to the ground on his back.

That was Corvo's moment, his best chance. He needed to finish the warrior while he was on the ground, but unfortunately Corvo had pushed so hard that when the warrior went down, Corvo too went stumbling forward. He was just about managing to keep his footing when a meaty hand grasped his left ankle and pulled. Corvo crashed to the ground with a yelp. He knew what was coming, and the moment his body hit the ground he forced himself to roll away from the fallen warrior, just as a mighty fist struck the ground where his face had been just moments ago.

The warrior roared in frustration and then started to get to his feet, but as he did so Corvo barrelled into him, sending them both to the ground again. Corvo had drawn his pugio and tried to stab the warrior in the neck as he collided with him, but for such a big man the warrior had incredibly fast reflexes. He managed to grab Corvo's wrist and divert the blade at the last moment. Instead of plunging into the warrior's neck as Corvo had hoped, the tip of the blade instead scored a deep gash across the man's left cheek, and blood was soon running into his straggly beard. The warrior roared with rage and threw Corvo off him as both men scrambled to their feet. Again the warrior was the fastest to react; he had soon retrieved his large sword and began to wave it around menacingly. Corvo glanced around, desperate for a weapon, but none were within reach. The warrior had begun to close in on him when a voice called out.

"Marcus!"

Corvo risked a glance to his left just as Atilus, covered in blood, tossed a pilum in his direction. Corvo reached out and caught it instinctively. It wouldn't have been his weapon of choice, but Atilus was an expert at this type of combat, and Corvo trusted his judgement. His reach would now be equal to or perhaps longer than the warrior's.

Corvo felt Atilus fall in beside him, also brandishing a spear.

"No! He's mine."

"Centurion … are you sure?" asked Atilus tentatively.

"Yes. Go help someone else." Corvo leaped forward and thrust the spear point at the tribesman several times, but the warrior avoided it.

He suddenly closed in on Corvo with great speed, swinging his sword in all directions. Corvo managed to duck or block most swings, but received a nasty gash on his left forearm. He glanced at the wound and cursed. The Germani warrior grinned, then attacked again. The first lunge was deflected by the javelin; the second struck Corvo's plated armour but didn't pierce it. Corvo knocked the man's sword arm aside and then swung the pilum like a club, the bottom end striking the warrior in the mouth and knocking his head sideways. The warrior reacted immediately and swung his sword at waist height, striking Corvo's left side and splitting his armour. It pierced his flesh, but the wound didn't feel too deep.

Corvo sensed rather than saw another swing coming his way, higher this time and aimed at his head. He ducked and at the same moment stepped forward, sliding his javelin between the warrior's legs. Then he pulled. The man's momentum combined with the spear tangled between his legs sent him crashing to the ground on his back. As he fell, he had the presence of mind to swing his sword, and it cut a deadly arc through the air at knee height. It had been Corvo's turn to react quickly, and he had jumped just in time to stop the blade severing his leg. As Corvo landed back on his feet, he grasped the spear with both hands and drove it as hard as he could into the warrior's chest. The Germani tried to swing the sword again, but Corvo quickly stood on the man's right wrist until the pressure forced him to release the sword. Corvo then quickly picked it up, marvelling at its weight and the strength of the man who had wielded it.

The Germani warrior tried to say something in his own language, but the words were cut off as he started to cough, thick blood spraying from his mouth. Corvo hefted the sword and prepared to put the man out of his misery, but then the big warrior gave one final cough, his body shook and he breathed no more. Corvo let out a long sigh of relief and looked at the wound on his arm. The bleeding was slowing but it would require stitches. The wound on his side was also steadily bleeding and would need attention.

Panic suddenly consumed him as he remembered Galba, Atilus and the legate were also fighting, though he could hear no noise. He twisted round, ready to help them, but all he found was a blood-soaked Atilus and a battered-looking Galba kneeling over the fallen body of the legate.

Corvo cursed and hurried over. "The legate — is he…?"

"No … he isn't … not yet, anyway…" replied the legate. "Remain here a while longer and that will change, I think."

Corvo didn't reply but looked at Atilus and then Galba. Both men shook their heads, meaning there was no saving the legate. Corvo looked down at his commanding officer and saw the multitude of wounds on his body. Many were superficial, but it was the slice across his stomach that would eventually kill him. The chieftain had carved the legate up and taken his time doing it.

"Don't look so morose, Centurion Corvo. At least I killed the bastard."

Corvo glanced to his right and saw the dead body of the chieftain. The battle was finally over. "We need to get you to the fort, Legate, where the medicus can see you."

"Don't trouble yourself, Centurion. It is done. I am … done. If you see … that old goat … Cornelius Arus again … tell him … tell him to watch over … Gaius."

"You can tell him yourself, Legate, once we find out where he's got to."

The legate chose to ignore Corvo's words of encouragement. They both knew they were hollow. "Thank you … for rescuing my son … so I might see him … one last time. I can die … a happy man."

"You're not dying, happy or otherwise, Legate." But even as he uttered those words, Corvo could see the light slipping out of the older man's eyes as his last shallow breath left his lungs. Corvo gently lay the legate's head on the ground and then brushed his eyes closed with his fingers.

The men who had pursued the fleeing tribesmen were now streaming back towards them. Some were even laughing as relief became the dominant emotion. Tribune Crispus was walking with Flavius, and they were sharing a story or a joke. When the tribune's eyes settled on the three men standing over his father's body, he rushed over to them and collapsed to the ground.

"No! No! No! How did this happen?" wailed the young tribune, fighting back tears.

"He died a true hero, Tribune. I saw him fall," said Atilus. "He faced their chieftain in single combat and overcame him but died of his wounds after his victory. You should be proud of him, as he was of you."

Corvo put a comforting hand on the young man's shoulder and then silently signalled for the other three men to follow him. They wandered off, leaving the man alone to grieve over his father's body.

"Did many get away?" Corvo asked Flavius.

"Only a few. They will not be a threat to Rome for at least a generation or two."

Corvo nodded approvingly. "Good. Lucius, if you could gather up the men left and see that the wounded get help, I will go and offer my gratitude to whoever leads the men that just saved our necks, even if they did leave it until the last possible moment to show up. Titus, Atilus, you both come with me in case I lose my temper and need dragging away."

"I think you would be better served seeking help for those wounds," said Atilus, looking at Corvo's arm and the blood seeping through his plate armour.

"It can wait. It's my temper I need help with right now."

The other men smiled and together the three of them strode off towards the bridge. Halfway across and flanked by the

241

legion standard-bearer in his leopard headwear and a number of officers, stood a broad-stripe tribune.

The three men came to attention in front of the tribune and Galba and Corvo saluted. Atilus did not, something which clearly did not go unnoticed by the tribune, though he chose not to question it at that moment.

"Tribune Helvius of the Twenty-Second?" asked Corvo.

"I am. Who in Hades are you and where is Legate Crispus?"

"I am Centurion Corvo of The Damned, this is Centurion Galba, also of The Damned, and this is Atilus." The tribune raised an eyebrow as if the name Atilus meant something to him, but again he chose not to pursue it. "As for the legate, I regret to inform you that Legate Crispus has fallen in battle. His body is over there where his son, Tribune Gaius Crispus, is currently mourning him."

"The legate is dead?" asked Tribune Helvius, staring past Corvo.

"I'm afraid so."

"How was this allowed to happen?" the tribune asked indignantly.

"We were hopelessly outnumbered and the legate chose to fight alongside his men like the true hero he was. There was no persuading him otherwise."

"This news will not be welcomed back in Rome. The emperor does not take kindly to his senior officers being killed."

Corvo thought differently. The legate himself had said that he had been sent to Germania to fail and that he had expected a visit from one of the emperor's assassins every day.

"Perhaps if you and your men had left the comfort of your fires and beds inside the fort and come to our aid earlier, much earlier, the legate would still be alive, as would many of my friends," said Atilus bitterly.

"How dare you speak to me in that manner, and why aren't you in uniform?" snapped the tribune, glaring at Atilus.

Corvo gave the former gladiator a withering look before turning back to face Tribune Helvius. "Atilus may have spoken out of turn, Tribune, for which I'm sure he's sorry —" Corvo tried to ignore Atilus' quiet snort of derision — "but what he says is true. If you and your men had come sooner, many lives could have been saved."

The tribune's anger seemed to quickly melt away, and his shoulders slumped. "I know, and I wanted to, but Legate Scipio of the Twentieth wouldn't let me march to your aid, even when Cornelius Arus turned up and begged for assistance. In fact, that just seemed to harden his resolve against helping you, and he ordered me not to cross the Rhenus to provide you with reinforcements. My men were on the point of rebelling over it. They wanted to march to their brothers' aid."

"So you disobeyed Scipio's orders? There will be consequences," said Corvo.

Tribune Helvius straightened his posture. "I have never disobeyed an order in my life."

"Until now?" interjected Atilus.

"No, I still haven't disobeyed an order. I was told not to cross the Rhenus to come to your aid under any circumstances, and I haven't. We fired arrows from our side of the river, and the men who launched pilums to break the tribesmen's final charge were positioned halfway across the bridge and no further. So you see, I didn't cross the Rhenus to help you." A small smile broke out on his face and Corvo matched it.

"Well, I thank you, Tribune Helvius. But I still think there may be consequences for you. Legate Crispus was right; you are a good and honourable man, and we are grateful."

"Really? He said that? I didn't think he liked me."

"He did."

"I was fond of him too, though I'd not known him long. The legions need more men like him and less like Scipio."

"Careful, Tribune, you're in danger of saying something that might put you on the emperor's list of undesirables," said Atilus.

The two men locked eyes, but then they both laughed.

"Well, we can't have that. Atilus? You were a gladiator once, were you not? And a good one too, if I recall. I saw you fight."

"Thank you. Yes, I was, but those days are behind me now."

"Now Atilus does his killing for The Damned, not for people's entertainment," added Centurion Galba.

"A pity. Anyway, as for Scipio, what can he do? Send me to a frozen wasteland full of barbarians? I believe I'm already there."

"Let's hope you're right," said Corvo. "Now, if you don't mind, Tribune, I'd like to arrange for my men to transport our dead and wounded to your fort, where they can receive proper treatment. What remains of my command would also be very grateful for a hot meal and a warm bed."

"And wine … lots of wine," added Galba.

"And not that watered-down piss either," said Atilus.

The tribune smiled. "Of course, we'll see what we can do. If your men can carry your dead and wounded across the bridge, my men will take over from there. Sorry, but it seems foolhardy to break my orders now," said the tribune apologetically.

"We'll get it done. Titus?"

"I'll see to it," said Galba, before striding back over the bridge and barking orders.

"You also look as if you are in need of some attention, Centurion," said Tribune Helvius.

"All in good time, Tribune," said Corvo. "Help my men first."

"Spoken like a true officer. Very well, I shall see you on the other side of the river, Centurion." Helvius turned and left the bridge, followed by the standard-bearer and his junior officers.

Corvo looked over to where Tribune Crispus was finally standing up, still staring at his father. He sighed and slowly started to make his way over to the young man who was now effectively his commanding officer.

CHAPTER 20

Cornelius Arus ceased his pacing up and down the atrium and clasped his hands behind his back. It wouldn't do to show these overpaid and pampered Praetorian Guards how nervous he was, though the smirks on their faces suggested they already knew. And why wouldn't he be nervous? Everybody who stood in that room waiting to see Emperor Nero probably felt the same way, given the unpredictable nature of the man. You could never tell which Nero you were going to encounter: the benevolent one or the spiteful one. Anybody who didn't feel anxious before such a meeting was a fool.

Arus tried to focus on the room's décor but found it too garish for his tastes. Busts of previous emperors and Mars the God of War were dotted around the room. In the most prominent position, next to the double doors leading through to where Emperor Nero currently held audience, was the largest bust of all. This, of course, was of Nero himself. It was a good likeness, even if it did make the emperor look younger and slimmer than he actually was. He had no doubt demanded this — the man was ever vain.

Arus tore his gaze away from the bust, lest his expression betray his feelings. Spies were everywhere and few of Rome's citizens could be trusted. Even the people Arus had travelled to Rome to seek help from on behalf of Legate Crispus had disappointed him and seemed changed. He no longer had faith in any of them. Anyone, it seemed, was willing to whisper poison in the emperor's ear about a friend or family member if it served their purpose. Perhaps someone had already said something about him and that was why he had suddenly been summoned to see the emperor.

Arus tried to quell the rising panic he could feel in his stomach. Whatever the reason for his summons, he would deal with it as best he could. There was no alternative. He just needed to keep his mind clear and remain focused.

He glanced down at the mosaic on the floor, which depicted Nero slaying some barbarians at the head of his legions — a battle that had never taken place. It was a mere figment of the man's imagination and ego. Arus was glad he was looking down, as he was sure his disapproval would be obvious to the Praetorian Guards who continued to watch him like a hawk.

For what felt like the hundredth time that day, Arus occupied his mind by trying to work out why the emperor had summoned him. That the emperor knew he was back in Rome was no surprise at all. One of his many spies would have noticed his covert arrival in the city the moment he walked through the gates — that was to be expected. They would also have attempted to follow him around the city to ascertain his reason for being back in Rome. Arus had anticipated this too and had taken precautions. Adept at working in the shadows and following people himself, he knew how to remain hidden. He was quietly confident that nobody who had tried tailing him would have been successful and that the identities of the people he had come to see remained concealed — for now, at least. He wondered if that was why he had been summoned. Perhaps the emperor was going to demand their names outright. Arus quickly considered which enemies or minor acquaintances he could sacrifice in the place of his real contacts. Then again, perhaps he should give their names up. After all, none of them had offered assistance, though in truth he knew they had wanted to, but were too scared for

247

themselves and the lives of their families. He was still considering this when the large oak doors swung open, and some obsequious minor dignitary stepped into the atrium, looked about and then summoned him loudly, even though he was the only man in the atrium save for the Praetorian Guards. Arus straightened his clothes, pasted a false smile on his face and followed the man into the emperor's audience chamber.

Nero was sitting at the far end of the room surrounded by about a dozen courtiers, sycophants who were smiling enthusiastically as the emperor recited a poem he had written. Arus had only caught some of it but still had to work hard to disguise his frown. What he had heard had been truly awful, but the people who Nero had surrounded himself with were pleading for more.

Nero smiled contentedly as the small crowd clapped upon the completion of his recital. Arus hoped his own smile, however false, remained stoically in place.

The emperor's gaze finally fell on Arus. "Ah, Cornelius Arus, what did you think of my latest modest poetry recital?" Every pair of eyes in the room settled on the newcomer.

"Your words are like honey from the gods, Imperator, a salve for sore ears and melancholy, and delivered with such eloquent poise. My only regret is that I was not present to hear the full rendition and was instead left to admire a bust of greatness rather than the man himself." Arus briefly wondered whether he had been too gushing in his praise. The emperor's expression gave nothing away and neither did the crushing silence in the room.

Arus needn't have worried. Nero suddenly broke into a huge smile and his cheeks coloured. "Thank you, Arus — finally, somebody who truly understands and appreciates my talents, unlike these fools." He waved his right hand dismissively towards the small group of people sitting around him. "Be gone from my sight. I wish to discuss matters with my friend Cornelius... We are friends, are we not, Cornelius?" The smile had disappeared.

"If you wish it, Imperator, I would be most honoured to be able to call such a talented and cultured man my friend. However, I fear I have little to offer our friendship in return," replied Arus as he watched the last of the sycophants disappear through the double doors, leaving him alone with the emperor, two Praetorians and a man he didn't recognise. He was dressed in a civilian toga, wore little jewellery and was around Arus' age. If it wasn't for his different coloured eyes, Arus would have only been able to describe him as non-descript. He was perfect material for a spy or master of spies. Arus' senses went on high alert. This was a rival — a man to be wary of. He suspected he knew his identity.

"Now, I'm not sure that's true at all, Arus," replied the emperor. "I think you have a lot to offer our friendship, and so does Darius here." Nero flapped a nonchalant hand in the direction of the other man.

"You flatter me, Imperator. As for Darius, I do not believe I have had the pleasure."

"What? Oh no, I suppose you haven't. Darius is my master of spies and keeps me informed of what is going on in my empire while I pursue the arts. It would not be fair of me to deprive my people of my poetry and music by being totally consumed by matters of state. This way, Darius deals with the more mundane matters while I write and recite."

"Of course," replied Arus. *So this is Darius, my nemesis.* "And how can I serve you, Imperator?"

The emperor picked up a lyre and began playing a tune he had composed himself. Arus briefly winced as the sound grated on his ears, and he was grateful the emperor was looking down and didn't notice. Darius, however, clearly had and was smirking.

The emperor put the lyre down, a look of disgust on his face, clearly not happy with what he had just heard.

"This won't do. I'm too distracted to focus on my musical talent."

"Would you like me to return another time, Imperator?" asked Arus.

"No. No, let's do this now, then perhaps I can get back to doing something useful. Now, Darius tells me you've been away on a little adventure." Arus couldn't decide if that was a statement or a question, but in the end he decided to remain silent. It was the right thing to do, as Nero soon resumed. "He says you've been to Armenia with your own little army to rescue Legate Crispus' son." The emperor paused. "Well? Is it true?"

"Yes, Imperator. The legate's son and a number of other men were being held captive by the traitorous Armenians in a desert fort. The legate knew that the Empire couldn't afford to send the legions to rescue them, and he didn't want to trouble you with such a trivial matter, so…"

"The rescue of his son was a trivial matter?" There was a glint of mischief in the emperor's eyes. He was not as stupid as people seemed to think, Arus decided.

"Not to the legate, Imperator, no, but to you who has all the matters of state weighing on your shoulders, yes, of course. He didn't want to add to your burden by bringing this matter before you," replied Arus.

"Instead he raised his own little army and sent them off to do his bidding?"

"Most of the men were the dregs of the Empire, Imperator, men that wouldn't be missed — gladiators, deserters, thieves and the like. Only a handful of the men were legionaries. The men's wages were paid by the legate himself, so there was no cost to the Empire."

"Yes, yes, I know all this. Darius has told me. Legate Livius Tullius also tells me that once they had rescued the legate's son and some more of my men, they helped in the defence of a fort until Tullius arrived. Is that also true?"

"It is, Imperator."

"That is to your and the other men's credit, Arus. However, are you aware that I consider Legate Crispus a danger to my throne?" From the corner of his eye, Arus saw Darius staring intently at him, assessing his reaction. He had to tread carefully here.

"Much has changed in the months we were away, Imperator, of that I'm sure. However, when I and the others left, we did so at the behest of a loyal Roman officer who wanted his son back but who didn't want to trouble the emperor he loved and served. I saw no traitor then, and although the legate is somewhat diminished from the man I last saw in Dacia, he is still a loyal Roman officer who only seeks to serve his emperor and Rome."

"You think I am mistaken or lying, perhaps?" Nero's eyes narrowed. Darius' smirk was back and although he couldn't see them, Arus sensed that the Praetorians were reaching for their gladii. His life was in the balance. He had to weigh his words carefully.

"I think you are neither, Imperator. However, I do wonder whether some of the intelligence you are being fed is inaccurate or perhaps serves another purpose." He glanced meaningfully over at Darius and saw the man bristle for a moment or two before his cold demeanour and neutral expression returned.

"Perhaps you are right," said Nero. "I will think on what you have said, and in the meantime Crispus can remain in the north, where he can do no harm ... to me, at least." Nero picked up his lyre and began to play it again. Arus was unsure whether that was his cue to leave and hesitated. Darius stepped out from the shadows and whispered something in Nero's ear before resuming his original position.

Nero sighed and stopped playing. "Oh yes, I have something for you to do, Arus."

"I am at your service, Imperator."

"I want you to go to Britannia with your men... What were they called again?"

"The Damned, Imperator. But with respect, they are not my men — Centurion Marcus Ovidius Corvo commands them."

"Ah, yes, The Damned — such a fanciful name." Nero chuckled. "And yes, I know all about Centurion Corvo — Tullius speaks very highly of him. Yes, I want you to travel to Britannia with ... The Damned."

"Britannia, Imperator?"

"Yes. Darius tells me there is trouble brewing, and I'm not sure that fool Paulinus is up to dealing with it. I need you and your men there to be my eyes and ears and to do whatever needs to be done."

"I apologise, Imperator, but I am not sure I fully understand what it is you want us to do."

"You act as a fixer for Legate Crispus, doing what needs to be done behind the scenes — things that the legate cannot be seen to do himself, perhaps?"

"I try to do whatever the legate asks of me, that much is true."

"Good. Then I want you to do the same for me, but on a bigger scale."

"I am honoured, Imperator, but forgive me … is that not what Darius already does for you?"

"In a manner of speaking, yes. But the Empire is vast, and enemies lurk in the shadows in every corner. Darius has more than enough work here in the city to do, rooting out plotters and traitors. He must remain here. I want you and The Damned to travel to Britannia and do whatever is necessary to prevent the province from deteriorating into open rebellion as Darius here thinks it might. It may have already done so. If that is the case and a rebellion has already started, you are charged with doing whatever is necessary to put it down. Do you understand now?" Nero fixed Arus with a hard stare.

"I do, Imperator, but…"

"Unless of course you would like to remain here and be considered a threat, like Legate Crispus?" Nero went on. Darius' smirk was back. Arus was trapped and he knew it.

"No, Imperator, of course not. I am yours to command. I was merely going to enquire about the chain of command."

"Governor Paulinus will be told of your arrival and will think he's in command, of course, but you will be largely autonomous. I want you and your men to fix problems before they arise and act independently — I don't want you involved in pitched battles or the like. He's got plenty of men for that, should the need arise. You will have authority to access and requisition everything you and your men need."

"So I and Centurion Corvo…"

"Corvo?"

The emperor's attention was starting to waver, Arus realised, his thoughts no doubt turning to music and poetry. He had already explained who Corvo was, and the emperor had claimed to be aware of him. "He is the commander of The Damned, Imperator. Legate Crispus merely sent me along as a fixer … if you recall?"

"Yes, yes, I know that."

"So I and Centurion Corvo report to Governor Paulinus, but if we think he's wrong or is not prepared to follow what we consider the best course of action, we can overrule him and proceed anyway?"

"There … you do understand, Arus."

Arus understood all too well. He understood that such a policy was going to lead to friction with the senior commander in Britannia and would at some point drop everyone in The Damned in the latrines.

"Yes, Imperator, I do."

"Excellent. Darius has already had the letters of authority drawn up bearing my seal, so whatever you need, you can have. Just don't fail me." He made to start playing his lyre again, but Arus gave no sign of departing. "There is something else, Arus?" he asked wearily. His attention and patience for such matters had clearly now expired.

"Forgive me, Imperator, but if I do this, Legate Crispus — if he has not already done so — may withdraw over the Rhenus with what remains of his men and will remain unharmed?"

"How dare you try and bargain with the emperor!" roared Darius, drawing the attention of the two Praetorians. "You forget yourself, Arus."

So he does speak, mused Arus.

"As do you, Darius," replied Nero, staring at Darius. "I do not need either of you to speak for me." He noticed the two Praetorians had their hands on their gladius handles and had taken a few steps forward, so he waved them back and they relaxed their stance. Darius looked abashed. "I do not bargain with anyone, Arus; you would do well to remember that in future. And if I command you and that band of ruffians you call The Damned to go to Britannia, you will do it, or I'll see you all crucified by sunset. However, as a gesture of goodwill and to demonstrate my benevolence, Legate Crispus may withdraw over the Rhenus with his men and resume command of his legion, but he is to remain on the frontier until I've decided whether he is a threat or not."

"Thank you, Imperator. I will leave for Germania at once."

"No need. Darius sent a rider as soon as you were spotted in the city. He should be with your men within a matter of days, bearing orders for them to march immediately to northern Gaul, where you are to meet them."

So I had no choice? thought Arus caustically. "Thank you, Imperator, that is most kind. The thought of several more long weeks in the saddle did not fill me with joy."

"There, you see, I am always thinking of my subjects. Do not try my patience again, however, Arus. Now go, before you completely drain all of my creativity, and send those other fools back in. Every genius deserves an audience." Nero began to play his lyre.

Arus saluted and turning sharply, hurried out of the room, the Praetorians opening the doors for him before following him out. Once the small group of sycophants had filed back in, cheering and clapping as they went, they shut the doors again. Arus let out a long sigh and then marched out without looking back. Behind him, Darius, master of spies, watched him leave.

EPILOGUE

Fort Voltera, Roman side of the Rhenus, early spring AD
60

"By the gods, just when you think this accursed land can't get any colder, it does," said Titus Galba as he downed the last of his wine.

"Missing the sweltering heat of Armenia, my friend?" asked Centurion Corvo mischievously.

"That place was too hot, hotter even than Tartarus, I wager. Why can't we ever be posted to somewhere with a temperate climate? Why's it always got to be ridiculously cold or stifling hot? What's wrong with Gaul or somewhere like that?"

"There's no fun left to be had in Gaul — Caesar saw to that. No, for excitement we've got to go to the far extremes of the Empire, not the safe and tame middle," answered Corvo.

"I'd be glad for a posting anywhere right now," said Flavius. "How long have we been here now? It feels like an age."

"I agree. It's been quiet since we crossed back to this side of the Rhenus, but it's also safer. No barbarians trying to chop my head off — I could get used to that. The defeated tribe has seeped away into their forest to lick their wounds, and no other tribes have risen up to support them."

"Well, we need something, or the men are going to start to melt away," said Galba.

"They already have," said Corvo. "A couple of freed slaves asked for their share of the silver and then left. Now that spring is here, more will follow their example. The mission is over, and they have done everything we asked of them, so we cannot blame them."

"It seems a real shame. We moulded them into a good group of men, tough soldiers. You'd think the Empire would have a use for us."

"Not all of us want to do Nero's bidding," said Atilus, speaking for the first time. "Some of us were just here for the adventure…"

"And to get away from people to whom you owe money, eh?" Corvo reminded him good-naturedly.

"Yes, that too in my case. There aren't many of my former brothers who would relish continuing to fight for Rome."

"Then you too will be off when the snows finally melt?" asked Flavius.

"Looks that way. With my friend Galba here I've nearly drunk the fort dry and have tried every whore. My pockets are fat with legionaries' wages — all won fairly at the gaming tables, I assure you — and I grow bored. I need adventure, excitement. I am no legionary content to sit around, grow fat and draw my wages."

"You could always return to Rome and pay off your debts," said Flavius.

Atilus burst out laughing. "I'm going to miss your sense of humour, Lucius. Pay off my debts! That'll be the day."

"I thought Cornelius Arus would be back by now," said Corvo.

"He's not coming back. That much is obvious, even to me," said Galba. "He's eating himself fat in the warmth of Rome while we're breaking our teeth on rations and freezing our manhoods off up here in a frozen wasteland."

Corvo laughed. "And what of you, my friend? What will you do — return to the Sixth? They're probably back from Egypt by now."

"You never did tell us why you were on — what did you call it? — 'administrative duties' in Rome while your legion was sunning itself in Egypt," said Flavius. "Now would seem as good a time as any to remedy that."

"Not until my tankard is filled," said Galba, looking around and eventually catching the eye of a serving girl. She was a lovely-looking young blonde woman from one of the local tribes allied with the Empire and was constantly having to fend off the attentions of just about every legionary in the fort.

When she returned with their drinks a short while later, Flavius looked at Galba and said, "Well, Titus? We're waiting." They all sat back in expectation of a great story.

Galba sighed and then took a long sip of his wine. "Oh, very well. There was this girl, and…"

"I knew it!" interrupted Atilus.

"Do you want me to tell you or not?" snapped Galba.

"Please, by all means," replied Atilus, holding his hands up placatingly.

The door to the mess hall had opened, letting a flurry of snow and a bitingly cold wind blow in, drawing the wrath of the men sitting closest to the door. The young legionary who had come in quickly shut the door behind him, apologising as he did so. He looked around the large mess hall, as if searching for somebody. Corvo watched him curiously.

The legionary had approached a table of soldiers and seemingly asked them something. The oldest of the group, a junior centurion, stood up and looked around until his gaze settled on the table where Corvo and his friends sat. He then pointed in their direction. The young legionary appeared to thank the centurion and after straightening his posture, he hurried over to where they all sat. He glanced around the table and seeing that at least three out of the four men sitting there were officers, he came smartly to attention and saluted.

"Now, what have we here?" asked Flavius.

"A shiny new soldier, by the looks of it," said Atilus.

"By the gods, our soldiers get younger every time I see one," said Galba.

"No, you're just getting older, my friend," said Corvo.

"And fatter," added Atilus.

Galba looked mortified and placed both hands on his belly. "It's muscle, that's all."

"You keep telling yourself that, Titus, and you'll be fine," Atilus replied with a smirk.

The young legionary looked uncomfortable, seemingly unsure whether he should interrupt or remain silent until addressed. Corvo decided to put him out of his misery.

"What do you want, Legionary?"

"I'm looking for Centurion Corvo, sir."

"Well, you've found him. What do you want with me?"

"I have a message for you, sir."

That caught the attention of everybody around the table and all conversation ceased. They hadn't received a message from anybody outside the fort since they'd been there. "Very well, let's have it."

The legionary began to search his person until he finally remembered where he'd stowed the message. He then withdrew it and passed it to Corvo.

Flavius let out a long, low whistle when he saw Nero's seal. "Looks like somebody's in trouble."

The legionary was still standing next to them. "You're dismissed, Legionary. Go and get yourself something hot to eat and a drink; you look frozen," said Corvo.

"Thank you, sir." He saluted and hurried away.

"So what does it say? Are you to be crucified?" asked Flavius, grinning as he watched Corvo break the seal and read the message.

"It's from the emperor. We are to march with all haste to a port in northern Gaul, where Arus will meet us. We have a new mission, which Arus will tell us about when we see him, but in the meantime I am to bring The Damned up to strength. I have the authority to requisition whoever and whatever we need on the authority of the emperor."

"I thought you said nothing happens in Gaul?" said Atilus.

"It doesn't," said Corvo, smiling. "That's why they're sending us to Britannia."

"Britannia?" the other three men chorused.

"So it would seem."

"What's in Britannia?" asked Atilus.

"Barbarians like yourself, rain and mist," replied Galba.

"You've been?" asked Flavius.

"No, but some of the men in the Sixth had, and none of them had anything good to say about the place."

"That's encouraging," said Flavius mournfully.

"Cheer up, men. At least it will be a change of scene. Now, drink up, we've got a lot of planning to do and very little time, so this is what I'm thinking…"

A NOTE TO THE READER

Dear Reader,

The first thing to say is thank you once again for taking the time to read *Forests of Death*, the second book in the Legion of the Damned series. I hope you enjoyed it. In the third book, *Islands of Mist*, Centurion Corvo and his comrades move from the snowy forests of Germania to the damp and misty islands of Britannia where rebellion is brewing under Queen Boudica of the Iceni.

I have always loved military history, and it was the only subject that I ever excelled in at school. It didn't matter what period my studies covered I enjoyed it all, but it was Roman history which always captivated me the most. The Roman Empire arguably began its decline in the early fifth century, their legions making a hurried departure from our shores in AD410. Roman historians such as Tacitus, Suetonius, Cassius Dio and of course Julius Caesar left some good, albeit biased accounts of the pivotal events in Roman history, but they are few and far between, which leaves a wealth of opportunities for the fiction writer.

I wanted to exploit some of these opportunities and write something different to the norm and hence the Legion of the Damned was born. In this book, Corvo and his disparate band of ex-gladiators, freed slaves, criminals and deserters end up in the cold and dangerous snow-covered forests of Germania, north of the Rhenus (Rhine). Germania and the tribes who lived there, particularly north of the river, were a constant thorn in the side of the Roman Empire. Few chose to side with the Romans and be assimilated into the Empire and even those the Romans considered conquered could not be fully trusted. The betrayal by Arminius of Publius Varus and the destruction of three Roman legions in the Teutoburg Forest in AD9 is testimony to that. It seemed only right then that at some point Corvo and his men should experience the harsh conditions and fearsome warriors that lived in that region.

Whilst some of the people and events depicted in my books were real — Emperor Nero for example — the vast majority of the characters and events are fictitious. I am, after all, a storyteller.

To the best of my knowledge, the vast Roman army did not possess a force of expendables such as the Legion of the Damned. Quite the opposite in fact, because initially only property-owning Roman citizens aged between 17 and 45 were allowed to join the legions. As the Empire's borders expanded and their enemies on the other side increased, however, these rules had to be relaxed, or the Empire risked being overrun because of what we would today term as snobbery.

If you have enjoyed reading this book and have a few moments to spare, I would be truly grateful if you could write a review on **Amazon** and **Goodreads**. Reviews are the lifeblood of authors nowadays and are crucial for our success. I am also always keen to connect with my readers, and you can contact me via **Facebook**, **Twitter** or **my website**.

Thank you once again and I hope you join the Damned as they undertake their next impossible mission in *Islands of Mist.*

Jeff Jones

www.jeffjonesauthor.co.uk

Sapere Books is an exciting new publisher of brilliant fiction and popular history.

To find out more about our latest releases and our monthly bargain books visit our website:
saperebooks.com

Printed in Dunstable, United Kingdom

71704942R00150